THE HERO INSIDE

Nicolai Schümann

First paperback edition November 2020

Book design and illustrations by Maite Lantaron

Set in Merriweather and Montserrat

The book is registered as follows:

Schümann, Nicolai
The Hero Inside
ISBN 978-1-8383168-9-1 (paperback)
ISBN 978-1-8383168-8-4 (hardback)
ISBN 978-1-8383168-7-7 (ebook)

Printed in the United Kingdom

Published by Universal Storyteller
www.universalstoryteller.co.uk

This book is dedicated to all heroes and heroes-in-waiting out there.

... and to my uncle Gunter, who was one of my first heroes.

ABOUT THE AUTHOR

Nicolai Schümann is a lecturer, trainer, and entrepreneur. He runs the storytelling agency Universal Storyteller and co-founded the lifestyle brand Alice's Pig and the innovation agency Horizon Innovation Lab. Also, he lectures at CASS Business School and gives workshops and training for corporate clients and start-ups. Nicolai writes, and mentors, and lives a curious life in and out of South London.

TABLE OF CONTENTS

PART III – ID, the instinctual desirer

PART IV - FRIENDS AND COMPANIONSHIP

INTRODUCTION

It was a sunny and unusually hot Saturday in early May, which I vividly remember because it was also my birthday. A rather dull birthday, as it turned out, since I had to work and most of my friends had left the city to enjoy their bank holiday at the sea.

But on that day, a seemingly innocuous question by one of my students sent me on a writing journey that would last for the next three years.

The day started with me teaching my "Storytelling in Business" class to some smart and ambitious post-graduate students at Cass Business School in London, England. As always, I presented my class with the Hero's Journey to explain and illustrate the concept of story structure.

The Hero's Journey, a term coined by mythologist and historian Joseph Campbell, is proof that all stories and myths around the world have basically the same underlying structure. Campbell calls it the monomyth. I finished the lesson that day with a feeling of satisfaction, for I thought my class had enjoyed it and grasped the basic concept of story structure.

But then, after the lesson, an inquisitive student from a small village in West Ireland came to me. This was Molly. With her long, curly red hair and dungarees embellished with 1970s flower prints, she looked more like an art student than somebody embarking on a business career.

In any given class, I always have a handful of students who are more curious than the rest, who want to get to the bottom of things, who keep on asking and asking until they fully understand. Teachers love them, but they can likewise drive us crazy. Molly was one of those.

Molly had already caught my attention in an earlier class when we discussed career aspirations and what students wanted to do after getting the MBA. I usually would get professions such as investment banker, consultant, and controller high up on the wish list.

But Molly said she wanted to be a penguin counter for a while. "A– what?" I asked her.

She said that nature societies sometimes look for penguin counters. Those are people who are willing to be locked in a cabin in Antarctica over a long winter season and count penguins to keep track of any changes in their population. Molly was convinced that not only was this a good thing to do, but it would also give her some quality time for introspection because she wouldn't have to deal with other people for a while.

Penguin counter was undoubtedly the most interesting job aspiration I had heard from a business student. I'm still puzzled as to why Molly chose to pursue a business degree in the first place.

But on that day, my birthday, Molly didn't want to discuss her future plans about Antarctica with me. She wanted to know what a hero was. She said she understood the Hero's Journey and all that but still didn't get what the main characteristics of heroes really are. Molly was especially eager to find out if, and how, she could apply those heroic character traits to her own life.

I wasn't sure if I had the right answer. But as a teacher, I didn't want to be exposed as not knowing, and I wanted to give her at least some kind of advice. So I said, "Well, first we have to embark on that Hero's Journey. Then, if we play it right, we'll be transformed to the better in the end."

Molly was not happy with my response. "But what *are* the character traits of a hero?" she asked. "Is there any psychological concept that can help us understand those heroic traits? And more important: Is there any way of becoming more heroic?"

We ended up in a long discussion about business ethics and how we need more heroes in leadership positions who would prevent things like the financial crash or the Enron scandal from happening again. We were so deeply engaged in theorizing that the next thing we noticed, it was an hour later, all the other students were long gone, and it was starting to get dark.

(From that day on, I introduced heroism and ethics in business as an integral part of my class– thanks, Molly!)

At the end of that long and fruitful conversation, it hit me that I still did not have a good response to Molly's initial inquiry about the character traits of a hero. I promised her that I would do some research and get back to her with an answer to her question.

I never did. I did not find an answer out there that fully satisfied me. I found a lot of stuff about the Hero's Journey and a few research papers about some typical hero traits, and there were academic debates about whether heroes are made or born.

But there wasn't anything on what I was looking for: a compendium of the most frequent heroic traits, along with a psychologically founded explanation of why those traits are useful and how we can adapt them to our own lives.

That's why I decided to write this book. Ideally, I hoped to fill it with exciting stories of both fictional and real-life heroes to illustrate the concepts I taught. For the next three years, I researched facts, interviewed people, and watched many heroic stories. Here are the results.

Molly, this book is for you. I hope you will find the answers to your questions within these pages. Apologies for the long wait.

What this book is not

This is not an academic study

Though I tried to ensure that all identified psychological traits of heroes and their advantages are backed up with numerous academic studies, overall, I provided more of a universal overview of all character traits rather than dissecting only a few topics with academic research and rigor.

(I made the last sentence extra-long to please academics. May all the academics I interviewed for this book forgive me, and I hope everyone enjoyed the read anyway.)

This is not a self-help book

I don't believe in self-help books. They try to offer quick and simple solutions for the very complex beast called life. I believe in getting inspired by stories and the "ripple effect" heroic tales inspire; ripples that are created when people learn from example and pass on their good deeds. Then those good deeds are further passed on and will eventually create an infinite loop of good deeds. If this book creates only one tiny little ripple, its mission is fulfilled.

Methodology

First, I analyzed hundreds of popular movie heroes over all genres, as well as more than a hundred real-life heroes. I picked the heroes who were scoring highest on popularity lists, assuming that most people would be able to relate to them.

Then I isolated the thirteen most frequent character traits that I found.

Next, I researched each of those traits' psychological benefits and how they can be applied to real life.

Along my journey, I also did quite a bit of primary research. I talked to hero experts and psychology academics as well as practitioners around the globe.

Please note: Not all characteristics are present in all heroes, so, don't assume that you must possess all thirteen characteristics to be a hero. Regard this book more like a wedding buffet; take what you like and leave the rest on the table.

Why movies?

I researched and analyzed the character traits of heroes from three different sources: movies, novels, and real life. In this book, I focus on examples from popular movies for one simple reason: Popular movies make great examples because so many of us have seen them and can relate to them.

Spoilers

Yes, there will be spoilers in the book as I give away the endings of some of the movies I discuss. Please accept my apologies. I had to do it to provide the right context. But I did try to pick only movies that are so widely known and talked about that most people have already watched then. And if not, go and watch them anyway. It's worth it even if you already know the ending.

Organization of this book

The ancient Greeks thought that all people were actors in the drama of the gods above. For psychologists, we are simply actors in the drama of our minds, pushed by our animalistic desires and pulled by our moral and societal conscience. Thus, underneath the surface, our personalities are represented by the constant power struggles deep within us.

According to the psychoanalyst Sigmund Freud, we are all three personalities in one: EGO, SUPEREGO, and ID.

The EGO is the organized part of the personality structure. EGO keeps the ferocious desires and lusts of the ID in check and is controlled by the morals of the SUPEREGO.

It is fair to say that the EGO works as an arbitrator between the SUPEREGO and the ID, because the SUPEREGO and ID typically have conflicting plans. This means there is a lot of mediation work to do for the often-overwhelmed EGO.

Whereas the SUPEREGO strives to act in a socially appropriate manner, the ID is wild, hedonistic, and demands instant self-gratification.

Whereas the SUPEREGO controls our sense of right and wrong and responsibly reminds us of our guilt and shame, the ID works purely off the pleasure principle in a dark and uncontrolled part of our psyche.

Each of these personalities has its very own idea of what the outcome of the story should be. Their struggles are fueled by powerful motives, and each one is out for itself.

The character traits I have analyzed are sorted into these three dimensions:

The organized and realistic ones, like proactivity and positivity, are found in the EGO part.

The more universal moral traits, like responsibility and purposefulness, are described in the SUPEREGO part.

The hidden, impulsive character traits like curiosity and shadows are reflected in the ID.

0. WHAT IS A HERO?

...or why we need to push the bell curve to the right

Who is and who isn't a hero lies mainly in the eye of the beholder. According to a recent study by Scott T. Allisson (1), most people called one of their close relatives their personal hero. Relatives were closely followed by real-life heroes like Martin Luther King, Jr., and fictional heroes like Batman.

Whoever our personal hero might be, there is no doubt that heroes and their stories have taught us lessons since the dawn of history. From the times of cave paintings, the tales of heroes have determined the norms and rules of humanity. They serve as a warning against external forces, and they help to shape our identities.

The definition of what a hero is, varies widely out there. But one thing is apparent: Heroes move us. Heroes lift our spirits, our dreams, and our ambitions. We identify with them, we want to be with them, we want to be like them, and we want to follow their journey and their example.

Heroes challenge our world view because they often do things we thought could not be done. Heroes and their stories have always had a significant impact on the way we think, act, and live. Oscar Wilde was right when he said, "Life imitates Art far more than Art imitates Life." Heroes provide us with good examples and offer fresh ways of looking at old situations. Thus, they inspire us to embark on new journeys to follow their good deeds.

Origins

Historically the English word "hero" is derived from the Greek word *hērōs*, which literally translated means a protector and defender. People may traditionally associate a hero with a strong male character, but in fact, the first and original hero in Greek mythology was a woman named– well– Hero.

Hero was a priestess serving the goddess of love herself, Aphrodite. And Hero was the protagonist of a tragic, forbidden love story a là ROMEO AND JULIET. Hero had a secret lover, Leander, who swam every night from Asia to Europe to be in her arms and was guided only by a little lamp Hero would put up on a tower. That happy arrangement abruptly ended one day when Leander was caught in a storm and died. Our original Hero was so saddened by his death that she drowned herself.

This Greek myth represents one of the most essential character traits of a hero: They do not hesitate to sacrifice their own life for a higher ideal– for something bigger than themselves. In Hero's story, it was love.

There are fine lines between altruism, compassion, and heroism. People who are altruistic and compassionate act voluntarily in service or defense of others without expecting anything in return. People who act heroically do the same but go a step further: they act even when the personal risks and costs to them are clearly recognized.

Heroes almost always commit to moral pursuits. If they do not do so at the beginning of their journey, they do so at the end. Often, they start their journey as underdogs, and we sympathize with underdogs who struggle to achieve a moral goal.

Misconceptions

There are some common misconceptions about heroes. Many people intuitively imagine heroes as superhumans with super-strength, who are perfect, and free of any flaw.

But mostly, it is quite the opposite. Like all of us, heroes do have flaws and weaknesses, shortcomings, and fears. Most heroes are quite ordinary people. It is their deeds which are extraordinary.

A heroic life is not an easy one. Heroes often have to go through hardship, suffering, and setbacks. Heroes remind us of the duality of life: In every fully lived life, there will be joy and sorrow, beauty and horror, success and failure.

And, as we will see later in this book, it is suffering that can eventually transform ordinary people into heroes. The label "Hero's Journey" is misleading in that respect because at the beginning of the journey, there is no hero. There is an ordinary person who embarks on a journey, and that person only transforms to a hero through the hardships and challenges that must be overcome along the way.

Changing the bell curve

One key takeaway message is that heroes possess the courage and moral rectitude to resist the social pressures that promote immorality.

The famous psychologist Philip Zimbardo, who has long researched the good as well as the evil in humans, argued that "The opposite of a hero is not a villain, but a bystander." A bystander is somebody who could have stepped in to help but didn't.

According to Zimbardo's research, and using the bell curve of humanity, it is the villains and the heroes who are the outliers. (2) Few people do evil, and even fewer act heroically. The big middle part of the curve represents the vast majority of the population who are technically neither heroes nor villains. Zimbardo calls them "reluctant heroes" or "heroes-in-waiting." They often refuse the call to adventure and, by not stepping in when something bad happens, passively support evil activities.

Imagine we could move the bell curve just a tiny bit to the "good" side. Imagine we could get more people into action and inspire them to be heroes. That would make the world a better place indeed.

So, our journey begins. Let's take a close look at the main character traits of heroes and what we can learn from them.

PART I

EGO

the organized, realistic agent

1 PROACTIVITY

...or why all success is by a winding stair

Imagine a young archaeologist in the 1930s who only just escapes a booby-trapped temple in Peru; almost gets killed by the guy he thought was his partner; is chased and shot at by a native Indian tribe; but gets away in a water plane at the very last second.

After a short visit to his teaching position at a New England State college, he travels to Nepal; fights some villains in a tavern; travels to Cairo to free his kidnapped friend; steals a precious Ark from the Nazis; destroys their flying wing; and boards a tramp steamer to take the Ark to London.

From there, it only takes another thirty minutes of screen time, which includes a lot of fighting and dying, for the archaeologist to deliver the Ark to the government in Washington DC—where the priceless Ark is promptly put away and forgotten in an obscure storage facility.

This is a brief summary of RAIDERS OF THE LOST ARK. The young archaeologist is Indiana Jones himself, one of the quintessential fictional heroes of our time.

Take note of what might be Indiana Jones's biggest virtue: proactivity. He constantly makes decisions and takes action. He constantly *does* things. This is one trait that all heroes have in common: They are proactive and constantly *do* something. They always make decisions and take action, all the time. They do and do and do.

Proactivity is not exclusive to bold action heroes like Indiana Jones. Likewise, the heroine and truth-finding lawyer Erin Brockovich is constantly acting and working through countless files and questioning people to get to the bottom of injustice. So is Bob Woodward, the investigative journalist and real-life hero who brought us Watergate. Why is that?

If we don't do anything, nothing ever happens

Part of the answer comes from my grandfather. He always said, "If you don't do anything, nothing ever happens." Sounds obvious? Definitely, but there is a lot of wisdom in it. Proactivity is the beginning of everything. Things only start moving when somebody decides to act.

Imagine a story with a hero who doesn't do anything and can't make any decisions. That would be the story of somebody procrastinating on a sofa for two hours, thinking about what he might want to do. Wouldn't be the most exciting movie, we must agree.

Just imagine the opposite of proactivity. Imagine that some of our archetypical heroes had decided *not* to act. Imagine that Indiana Jones had stayed in his classroom instead of chasing the lost Ark. Imagine that Luke Skywalker had ignored the call to adventure and stayed on his home planet.

Would their lives have been happier? Maybe. But two things are certain: Their lives would have been a lot less exciting, and they would not have had the chance to grow and change into a larger self. They would not have become heroes.

Also, the Nazis would have found the formula for eternal life, and Darth Vader would have taken over the faraway galaxy. In these stories, humankind would have ended in complete misery if Indy and Luke hadn't decided to take action.

Why we often *do not* act

A lot of us avoid making decisions or taking action on many occasions. Let's take a deeper look into the psychology of why that happens.

Here is an interesting fact: Many people think that *not* taking action is the safer option. I can assure you that this is, in almost all situations, wrong.

Think about it. If we make a decision, even it turns out to be a big mistake, we at least learned something. More importantly, we have a result we can work with. If we take no action at all, we will remain in a limbo where nothing ever happens.

There is this thing with perfection. We often don't take action because we want to have a perfect plan and perfect conditions before we start. But rest assured that there is no such thing as perfect. Just begin and accept that we will make some mistakes along the way. Those mistakes won't make us look foolish; only pretending to be a flawless natural-born authority on all things will do that. Or is there anybody who never cracked a joke about Chuck Norris?

The curse called procrastination often prevents us from taking action. We all know it; we all have been there. But why do people procrastinate?

Well, procrastination can be a very useful psychological shelter for many of us. It is easier to continue business as usual and not leave our fluffy comfort zone. But that cozy shelter can come at a high price. If we do not take action, the losses will only accrue, and the opportunities might fade.

Procrastination, at its core, is nothing but the confusion of pain and pleasure, where we gain short term pleasure for long term pain. Not a very attractive deal, is it? But the sooner we act, the smaller our potential losses are, and the sooner we will have a result we can work from– even if the result means temporary failure.

This leads us to the next reason: We often procrastinate because of the paralyzing fear of failure. How do we overcome that fear? Just do it. Literally. Start anything, and the fear vanishes eventually. Think about it: The first step is always the most frightening. Once that is done, we come into momentum, and every next step will be less fearful.

The best results are often on the other side of fear, as we will see in the chapter titled "Fear." Stick to the words of the philosopher Ralph "Where's Waldo" Emerson: "Always do what you are afraid to do."

Beware of the endowment effect

We may avoid action because we tend to cling to the status quo and resist change. Behavioral economists call this phenomenon the "endowment effect," and means that people place greater value on things they do have than on things they don't have.

In other words, we prefer the "what is" to the "what might be." Again, this bias to the status quo is a nice little shelter that leaves us in our comfy comfort zone.

This is why people so often stay too long in bad jobs or toxic relationships, rather than stepping away into the unknown. We might not be very happy with what we have, but at least we know it and have some control over it; other options could be so much worse.

Sometimes we refuse to believe something *is* broken and continue to live a sheltered life in denial– until things spiral into a disaster.

Is there are a risk of failure if we leave our current state and step into the unknown? Absolutely. But the potential upside is so much bigger. If we never try, we have failed by default. As the eccentric grandfather in LITTLE MISS SUNSHINE put it wisely: "A real loser is someone who's so afraid of not winning he doesn't even try."

Assuming we don't operate a nuclear power plant for a living, we can instill a bit more liberty and experimentation into our day-to-day lives.

Think of Luke Skywalker again. He left his family home and the comfort of his little igloo to go on an epic adventure. But after many near-death experiences, he was rewarded with the glory of the galaxy. The moral here is: if we want to find the princess, we have to leave our home planet (and preferably come into possession of a lightsaber along the way.)

The cost of doing nothing can have severe long-term effects, no matter how alluring it might look in the short term.

Think about it. Looking back at our lives, what do we regret most? I'll bet it is mainly the things we haven't done rather than the mistakes we made.

Regret from failure fades quicker than inaction

Research by psychologists suggests that regret from failure is relatively short term and quickly fades (3). In contrast, we experience far more long-term regret over things we did *not* do. This is a big lesson for all of us: We have to try, even if we fail. The chances that we will be miserable and regretful in the long term will be so much lower.

In fact, heroes experience far more defeat than those who are not successful. A lot of us get knocked down once or twice and give up. Heroes get knocked down over and over and over again, but they keep bouncing back and keep moving forward.

Remember Rocky, in the boxing saga of the same name? In only two hours, that guy fails probably more times than the rest of us ever will during our entire lives. He gets knocked down over and over again. He sees his opponent double, he pisses blood, and he's booed by a hostile crowd every time he tries to get up again. But up he gets, over and over again, and he moves forward no matter what.

Another fact to remember is that heroes make mistakes all the time– and if they can fail, so can we. Heroes often view failure as a minor detour, a little delay on their long journey, and nothing more than a bump in the road.

Give yourself permission to mess up

So, how can we approach new challenges and take action with confidence and without this paralyzing fear of making mistakes? There are two main lessons to be learned from heroes:

a) Don't give a shit about what others think.

b) Give yourself permission to mess up.

Has a hero ever held back for fear of what others might think? Hell, no! Just think of Rhett Butler's last words in GONE WITH THE WIND, before he rode off into a new adventure: "Frankly, my dear, I don't give a damn." If we constantly worry about what others might think, we end up living somebody else's life and not a very good one. Rhett learned that lesson the hard way by staying too long with a woman who never loved him.

When it comes to messing up, I want us to reflect on our own lives. Like everyone else, there was a time when we were a one-year-old toddler. In those days, we had no fear of failure, right? If we had been afraid to fail, we'd never have learned to walk in the first place.

Yet we always acted. We tried to walk and fell on the ground, but we got up and tried again and fell again and did that hundreds of times... until we finally walked.

What has changed now? Why do we fear failure and refuse to take action? Why do we consider failure to be negative as adults?

Often, we are not afraid of failure itself. Instead, we are afraid of being judged over our possible shortcomings, be it through societal norms, peer pressure, or comparing ourselves to others.

That doesn't make sense at all if we think about it. Failure is the only reason we are able to walk, talk, swim, or do anything else. Failure made us, not success. Success is the end result, but it is failure that brings us there. The good thing about repeatedly failing is that after a while, the number of mistakes begins to drop off, and the success rate begins to climb.

The purpose of challenges and obstacles is to prepare us with the skillset we need to achieve our goals. Failures and defeats are prerequisites for success.

We must awaken that little one-year-old hero inside ourselves that has zero fear of failure and wants to try to do everything regardless of potential consequences. Access that brave little person once again and get into action irrespective of looming failure. Heroes do.

"Do, or do not. There is no 'try'."

Heroes often put themselves in situations where they simply have to act. In story structure terms, this is called "the point of no return." Indiana Jones running away from a giant boulder; Luke Skywalker having the Stormtroopers behind him and a chasm in front of him; or Marty McFly accidentally travelling back to the 1950s and then having to find his way BACK TO THE FUTURE.

All heroes accepted the call to adventure, embarked on their journey, and found themselves in situations where they simply have to act. There is no room for contemplation or hesitation anymore. Action is critical.

Remember BUTCH CASSIDY AND THE SUNDANCE KID? Early in the movie, our protagonists are cornered by the posse high up on a mountain cliff with nowhere to escape other than a wild river fifty meters below them. What did they do? They jumped off the cliff and survived. Tough decision? Yes. Big risk of failure? Hell, yes, especially knowing that one of them cannot swim. But they did do *something*. The alternative would have been procrastinating and slowly starving to death.

Rick in CASABLANCA woke up from his lethargy and decided to help Ilsa get out of the country. Han Solo decided to stop being a smuggler and help the rebellion instead. They all made risky decisions and *did something*.

If we ever face a big hurdle in life, which gives us no other choice but to act and overcome, we should regard that as a blessing because it *forces* us to act.

In very tough situations, we will find a strength we didn't think we had. Women who give birth know this feeling only too well. We must create our own momentum. We must go to the point of no return; we must dive off the edge of that chasm!

But when is it the right time to go into action?

The answer comes from the movie DEAD POETS SOCIETY. Its hero, the English teacher John Keating, tries to enliven and empower his students at a stiff boarding school in the 1950s. In one scene, he has his students gaze at a gallery full of old black-and-white photos of ex-students who are long dead now.

He asks his students a question: "Did they wait until it was too late to make from their lives even one iota of what they were capable? If you listen really close, you can hear them whisper their legacy to us. Go on, lean in. Listen. You'll hear it. *Carpe*– You'll hear it. *Carpe diem...!*"

The lesson from Mr. Keating is: Do it today! We need to scrap our wish-list and replace it with a do-it-now list. Or, as the saying goes: The best time to plant a tree was twenty years ago. The next best time is now. *Now*.

In case we are stuck with two options, we are equally happy with and can't make a decision; just flip a coin. But make a decision and get into action. Accept the fact that a decision *for* one thing is also a decision *against* some other thing. Don't live in limbo.

We must never fail to act because we fear we might fail. Remember that the cost of not doing anything usually is much higher than the price of trying something.

If possible, do the most difficult part of the job first. Once we've climbed the big, scary first hurdle, our confidence is boosted, we achieve a nice momentum, and we are better prepared for the rest of the journey.

"All success is by a winding stair," said the philosopher Francis "Butty" Bacon. In other words, do what we never expected to do and let unexpected dramas and events take their course. Life has mostly different plans for us than we expected anyway.

Did a young farmer called Luke think he would have a pivotal role in a galactic battle? Definitely not– but he did things he didn't expect he would do and followed his path proactively into the unknown.

The credit goes to the one in the arena

Theodore Roosevelt himself put it very astutely:

"*It's not the critic who counts; Not the man who points out how the strong man stumbles, or where the doer of deeds could have done them better.*

"The credit goes to the one who is actually in the arena; Who strives valiantly; who errs and comes up short again and again; Who knows the great devotions, the great enthusiasms, and spends himself in a worthy cause. Who, at the best, knows in the end the triumph of high achievement;

"And, at the worst, if he fails at least he fails while daring greatly; so that his place will never be among those timid and cold souls who know neither victory or defeat."

Nothing to add, Teddy.

Be the one on the stage, not the bystander. Go out, make decisions, and do stuff. And do. And do. And fail. And fail again. Fail often. Heroes do. After all, mistakes make good stories.

In the end, we might not get what we initially wanted; but chances are so much higher that we will not regret what we did.

FOR THE IMPATIENT AND HURRIED

Three steps to be more proactive:

1. BREAK IT DOWN

If a big task seems to be too daunting, break it into little manageable chunks and work through them one by one. Entirely devoting yourself to the task at hand will normally shut out any larger worries.

2. FLIP A COIN

We are especially indecisive when confronted by too much information or too many possibilities, which is especially challenging in our modern world of abundance. If we have a hard time making a decision, it is a sign that the options we face have a fairly equal value. It is then important to: a) make a decision, and b) be fully committed to it. Rationally it might not be the perfect decision, but it is our decision. Once we fully commit to it, we increase its value by default.

3. DON'T GIVE A SHIT

It is impossible to please everybody all the time. Impossible. Stop thinking about what other people might think or expect from us and our actions. Instead, ask yourself what the right thing to do is... and then do it.

2 SELF-DETERMINATION

...or why rule-breaking means progress

It is a cold autumn day in 1959. Young students from elitist backgrounds reluctantly get ready for their final year at Welton Academy in Vermont. Welton is an all-male elite prep school known for its high standards and ancient traditions, including physical punishment by the strict headmaster.

One day Mr. Keating, their new English teacher, is introduced to them. Things take a completely different course from then on. Mr. Keating is a breath of fresh air, challenging existing rules and mindsets. He encourages his students to make their lives extraordinary instead of leading lives of quiet desperation.

His methods are as unorthodox as himself. He makes his students stand on their desks to demonstrate different ways to look at life; he makes them rip out the old-fashioned introduction in their poetry book; he invites them to find their very own walking style to encourage and foster their individualism.

Inspired by Mr. Keating, the students secretly form a poetry club to express themselves artistically and find their voices. Through their artistic doings, one of the students, Neil, finds his passion for acting and performs in a local Shakespeare production. However, his authoritative father drags him out of the theater, withdraws him from the school, and enrolls him in a military academy instead. In a moment of despair, unable to stand up to his father and without support from his weak mother, Neil commits suicide.

Mr. Keating is scapegoated for the incident and discharged from his job. However, his students give him a passionate and heartfelt farewell, and we can see that they are now ready to lead a more conscious and self-determined life from then on.

This is the story of the beautiful movie DEAD POET'S SOCIETY.

Mr. Keating is disobedient and unconventional and does not fit into the reactionary surroundings of 1950s private schools. However, he leaves a mark; his students are inspired by Mr. Keating and follow his unorthodox example. They not only liberate themselves from their conservative surroundings and start breaking norms, but they also become intellectually more curious. There is hope that they will live an authentic life.

Mr. Keating was a rule-breaker. So are most heroes out there. If they always stuck to rules and conventions, nothing would ever change.

Better to ask for forgiveness than permission

One of my early college professors once told the class: "It is easier to say sorry afterward than to ask for permission beforehand."

There is a lot of truth to that. If we always follow the rules, there is a real danger that we will end up in a homogeneous herd and only do and think what everybody else is doing and thinking. As a result, our lives might become more controlled by others than we ever wanted.

In this chapter, we focus on two things: Self-determination and the concept of rule-breaking, which often go hand in hand. As we will see, these are traits most heroes have in common.

Self-determination means one's life is determined by oneself without any external control. It means having the freedom to live the life one chooses.

Sounds pretty enviable, doesn't it?

However, like many good things, this is easier said than done. Here is the one thing that prevents us, more than any other, from determining our own lives and being our true selves: rules.

We are conditioned to belong

Rules are everywhere. There are social rules, hidden rules, and very obvious rules. There are rules which are wrapped up in codes of conduct and standards. On a macro level, there are state rules. These are usually called "laws."

Rules often draw an invisible line in the sand and determine who can belong to a certain group and who cannot. Rules decide who is in and who is out. Violating the rules means that we might be kicked out of a school, a private membership club, a gang, or a costume party. Not being included in something can create societal pressure.

If there is one thing people are afraid of, it's exclusion from a group. That's because, neurologically, we are hard-wired for personal connections. That is why isolation is used as a form of punishment in our society. In primary school, it is the "naughty corner." As a teenager, nothing feels worse than to be ignored by the cool kids in class. In prison, the biggest form of punishment is solitary confinement.

From early on, we are taught to belong. This is, of course, not a bad thing per se. However, often we are taught to fit in, keep our heads down, and not push any limits at all. In short, we learn not to question the rules.

Psychologist Clive Williams and other psychological theories have pointed out that from the age of six or seven, we learn to lie so as not to upset those we love. (4) Many of us have learned not to say what we want and break those unspoken rules to avoid rejection. But, of course, that comes with the price that we might end up living a life in the confines of other people's expectations and beliefs.

There will be times when those beliefs need to be doubted, when limits need to be pushed, and when rules need to be broken. Saying "no" after a lifetime of reluctantly saying "yes" can be incredibly liberating.

Break the eggs at the big end

Unfortunately, rules are often simply assumed and not questioned. We obey them without thinking, and they can hinder us from living to our full potential.

Sometimes we wonder why rules don't seem to be working all that well until Mrs. Rulebreaker or Mr. Renegade comes along and breaks the rules– and then suddenly things work a whole lot better. To create change or progress of any kind, we have to break some rules.

Think about it: Very often, rules are mere generalizations and designed to apply to most people in most situations. They may not fit our unique circumstances. In addition, rules are often dated and based on information available at the time the rules were set up. Just think of the controversial gun laws that still exist in the USA today, which were initially set up on, uh, December 15th, 1791.

Furthermore, there may be rules we have not agreed with from their inception. They may have been forced on us and might not be in line with our values. This is often the case because we disapprove of the authority that created those rules in the first place. For example, they might have been established by a morally questionable board of directors or, even worse, a sinister regime.

Never forget that rules are frequently set by people in power who have a strong interest in staying in control. If we are not a fan of the system that created the rules, we should ask ourselves if following them is the right thing to do.

And, of course, there are all those small unwritten rules and norms that exist within our circle of friends or at the company we work for– all those subtle codes of conduct that are so deeply ingrained in the culture that everybody blindly follows them, even though they often turn out to be complete nonsense if we look closer at them.

The egg war in GULLIVER'S TRAVELS illustrates well the idiocy of unquestioned rules. For decades, in the nation of Lilliput, people broke their eggs at the little end because their king demanded it so. One day, the Big-Endians rebelled against him because they wanted to break their boiled eggs at the big end, too. A war ensued. This fable might sound silly at first, but there is a lot of truth in it.

Pushing the limits gives us identity

We can see now that blindly following every rule in every situation is just– with all due respect– plain stupid.

If obeying rules can harm other people, then it might be best to bend or break those rules when appropriate. Heroes would. The more unnecessary rules we break, the more there will be a growing consciousness that life is full of potential instead of filled with limitations.

I have more good news for rule-breakers out there: Breaking rules can enhance creativity. Researchers from the Harvard Business School and the Marshall School of Business found out that the more creative we are, the more we break the rules; and the more we break the rules, the more creative we get. (5) Sounds like a circular fun ride, doesn't it?

If we happen to have teenage kids who break the rules FERRIS BUELLER -style... don't be too hard on them. Research from Arizona State University shows that minor rule-breaking in adolescence predicted a rather interesting occupation in adulthood: entrepreneurship. (6) If we want our kid to be the next Richard Branson, let him get away with some minor damage to our old-timer collection.

Of course, I am not advocating complete anarchy here. After all, rules and laws are part of the foundation of our society. Without a certain degree of obedience, there would be nothing but chaos. Without some stable values to follow, society cannot function. Laws or rules that protect other people from harm should, of course, not be broken at all.

But it is crucial to break the occasional rule, to question authority, and push the limits once in a while. It makes us human and can foster progress and change. Also, it will prevent the people in charge from becoming complacent and make them amend their rulebook for the better.

This is where a beautiful thing called self-autonomy kicks in. If we obey all the rules and don't even question them, we make ourselves dependent on others and do not leave our mark. But if we break them, we stand out and perhaps move closer to our authentic self. When we start being self-initiated and self-directed, there is a much higher likelihood that we will make things happen in life. ***Our*** things. In ***our*** lives.

Don't let other people's rulebooks affect the decisions we make or how we feel about ourselves. We must have the courage to stand up and be the champion of our own path, no matter how weird it may seem to society's neat little rules. It can take tremendous strength to go against common practices, but isn't that what a self-determined heroic life is all about?

Listen to Nelson Mandela: "I am the master of my fate. I am the captain of my soul." He was a real-life hero and lived a self-determined life, even though that meant spending 27 years in prison.

Rule-breaking heroes

Let's take a look at some movie heroes who broke the rules.

Take THELMA AND LOUISE, from the eponymous film. They take their revenge on a rapist; separate themselves from all social rules; and break various laws on their journey. Yes, they come to a tragic end, but they stay true to themselves and have a lot of fun along the way. They also became heroic icons to a generation of moviegoers.

Take the classic example of ROBIN HOOD, who famously stole from the rich and gave to the poor. He was an outlaw and rule-breaker par excellence and changed many lives to the good.

Take a more modern example: DIRTY HARRY. The "dirty" part in Harry is that he is not only a cop but an unforgiving vigilante. In order to get the bad guys, he breaks all the rules and even some laws he is supposed to uphold.

All classic detectives are rule-breakers, from Sherlock Holmes and Philip Marlowe to Jake Gittes in CHINATOWN. They all break rules and are disobedient in order to solve their cases, and they (mostly) put the bad guys behind bars. Our favorite secret agent, James Bond, and his American counterpart, Jason Bourne, are big-time rule-breakers.

Even more extreme examples are the superheroes who break social norms and laws as they take the law into their own hands to save the world.

Another classic example is the seminal movie EASY RIDER. The two protagonists reject social rules and go on a memorable journey to find their personal freedom. The character George wisely explains a sad truth: "Americans value freedom, but fear those who exhibit it."

The list goes on and on. Almost every movie hero of note is a rule-breaker at heart, be it Indiana Jones, Han Solo, Erin Brockovich, or any Bette Davis or Charlie Chaplin -type character. All of them deviate from the norm to achieve their noble goal.

Some of the most heroic rule-breakers come from real life: the whistle-blowers. They break the rules and laws to inform society about injustices, putting their lives at risk for the greater good. Often that means losing everything, including their personal freedom. But they do it anyway because it is the right thing to do. Just look at the fate of Edward Snowden or Chelsea Manning. Bless them.

Without deviating from the norm, there is no progress

I hope I've made my case that breaking the rules and being self-determined can be real assets to our lives. We should not devote our entire lives to doing what we think would please others or meet with their approval. Of course, there is nothing wrong with doing those things; the problem arises when we seek to do so only in an attempt to validate our self-worth.

In that scenario, there is a real danger that our self-worth will rise and fall depending on the good graces of others. Believing that we must constantly live up to someone else's rules and standards can drain our motivation and internal drive.

So, go out there and question authority. Break a few rules. Be a little naughty and disobedient. Ask "why?" a whole lot more. That is what heroes do.

Mindlessly obeying the rules can be a very convenient way to live our lives. We get clear instructions on what to do and what to think, and we don't have to take any personal responsibility for our actions. It's easy. We just do as we're told, and then we can justify all our actions with "I was just following the rules."

This is exactly what the Nazis said at the Nuremberg trials. Their defense was that they were merely carrying out orders from those above them. By using this defense, they attempted to remove the blame from themselves.

Think about it: Historically, most terrible things– war, genocide, and slavery– have resulted ***not*** from disobedience but from obedience. The political theorist Hannah Arendt was right when she said: "Nobody Has the Right to Obey."

Real-life heroes like Rosa Parks, Gandhi, and Martin Luther King, Jr. used civil disobedience and broke rules to change things for the good.

Frank Zappa prominently said: "Without deviation from the norm, progress is not possible." And Mr. Zappa was 100% correct. Progress always involves change, for things cannot get better when everything remains the same. A crucial prerequisite for change is often rule-breaking.

There have always been renegades and mavericks in history who broke the norms, challenged the status quo, and did something fundamentally different from what anybody else had ever done. Their actions often resulted in a leap of progress for humanity. Of course, such actions are not always obvious or straightforward but can be the only way for things to change.

Being conscious that there cannot be full security and certainty at any point in our lives anyway makes the notion of breaking the rules even easier.

Listen to the words of George Bernard Shaw: "The reasonable man adapts himself to the world; the unreasonable one persists in trying to adapt the world to himself. Therefore, all progress depends on the unreasonable man."

If that sounds too highbrow, here is a piece of more practical advice from Katharine Hepburn herself: "If you obey all the rules, you will miss half the fun."

Be self-determined. Break rules. Heroes do.

FOR THE IMPATIENT AND HURRIED

Three reasons why we shouldn't be afraid to break rules:

1. RULES ARE NOT UNIVERSAL

Mostly, rules are not universal. They are generalizations that may not be tailored to fit us or our specific circumstances. Therefore, blindly following every rule in every situation is not the smartest thing we can do.

2. RULES MAY KEEP US FROM DOING THE RIGHT THING

While blindly following the rules is the easy way, sometimes they stand between us and doing the right thing. In that case, we must always prioritize doing the right thing.

3. RULES MAY BE DATED

Rules are based on the available information at the time they're created but might be dated and not adjusted for today's circumstances. If we feel they're outdated, break them.

3 GRIT

...or why only giving up means failing

Rocky Balboa is a struggling amateur boxer living a dreary life in a working-class area of Philadelphia. The little money he makes comes from working as a debt collector for a loan shark.

But one day, his monotonous life gets shaken up and catapulted onto a new track. He is arbitrarily chosen to fight the reigning heavyweight champion, Apollo Creed, when the undefeated champion's scheduled opponent pulls out due to injury.

It is an impossible challenge, but Rocky is willing to beat the odds. He brings his body into shape with tough and unconventional training methods: He gets up at four in the morning, downs a pint glass of raw eggs, and runs through the ice-cold industrial streets of Philadelphia. Due to the lack of professional training equipment, he goes to a friend's meatpacking plant and punches restlessly into sides of raw beef until his hands are numb.

However, on the night before the big fight, the sleepless Rocky visits the empty boxing arena and self-doubt kicks in. He is intimidated by the vastness of the place and loses confidence in himself. He doesn't think he will ever be able to beat the champion; but he does promise himself that he will not give up, no matter what.

During the big match, it soon becomes obvious that Apollo is by far the better boxer both technically and physically. But Rocky fights back with all he has; every time he gets knocked down, he gets up again, over and over again.

Later in the fight, Rocky's face has been hit so often that it resembles a cauliflower. He starts seeing his opponent double and can't feel his legs anymore. Every time he gets knocked down, the only thing he hears is the faint noise of the hostile crowd booing him. Ordinary people would rather die than keep getting up to fight a seemingly invincible opponent. But Rocky gets up anyway. Over and over again. And he keeps on fighting with all that is left in him.

In the last round, Rocky is slumped on the stool in his boxing ring. His eyes are so swollen from repeated blows to the face that he cannot see anything anymore. His trainer winces at his sight and is ready to throw in the towel to admit defeat. But Rocky begs him to open his eye. Reluctantly, the trainer slits Rocky's swollen eyelid and drains the blood from it, taking the swelling down enough to let Rocky open his eye and see.

Just barely able to see or stand, Rocky stumbles through the last round against an equally battered champion. As the final bell rings, the two fighters are locked in each other's grip, and each one promises they will never fight the other again. Rocky becomes the first boxer ever to go the distance against the reigning champion, Apollo Creed.

Rocky was inferior in every single aspect, but there was one thing he had more of than most other people: grit. He simply refused to give up.

This is the story of the first ROCKY movie from 1976.

A good story is about duality

If we aim high, we will be knocked down often. Better be prepared for setbacks and disappointments. And rejection. A whole lot of rejection. We will have to go into the rough to keep the game interesting.

A good life, like a good story, is about duality and conflict. There is both joy and suffering. Without the downs, we wouldn't appreciate the ups. Often, we have to accept short-term pain to achieve long-term contentment. The exciting bit is that we most often achieve our goals, not through talent, virtue, or luck, but through simply not giving up.

Some call it perseverance. Others call it resilience. I'll use the short and punchy expression: grit.

A simple definition of grit would be maintaining effort and working towards a goal over a long time, despite failure, adversity, and plateaus in progress. All heroes possess a certain degree of grit; if they didn't, their heroic journey would end prematurely.

The key is to go the distance. People with grit keep their chin up and maintain their determination and motivation towards very long-term goals, despite the challenges and setbacks they encounter along the way. We can choose to give up or we can choose to keep going. Life is a marathon, not a sprint.

Excellence takes time and persistence

So, what are the advantages of grit? The University of Pennsylvania's Angela Duckworth wrote a seminal book about grit. (7) According to her psychological research, there is a strong connection between grit and general well-being, optimism, and life satisfaction.

And people scoring high on the grit scale are much less likely to take their own lives. Why? Because they still have things to do and things to fight for.

Grit also makes us more trustworthy because other people know we will not give up when the going gets rough. We might even make unexpected discoveries because we will dig deeper and go further than other people.

Most striking, grit is strongly related to improved performance in any field including career success. According to Duckworth's research, grit is a far better predictor of long-term success than either talent or strong cognitive abilities.

Remember Malcolm Gladwell's 10,000-Hour-Rule? This rule says that we can master almost anything if we are willing to put the hours into it. A *lot* of hours– 10,000 hours, according to Gladwell. (8) It is perspiration, not inspiration, that makes the difference.

Think about this analogy for a moment. Most great endeavors are like swimming across a big lake. In the beginning, when we get into the water, there is quick progress. The trees behind us quickly get smaller, and we feel we've made a reasonable distance towards our goal. The final stage seems to happen quickly, too. When we are close to the other side of the lake, the trees again get big very fast and when we get out of the water– if we are lucky– there is a cheering crowd waiting, and somebody hands us a medal.

But there is also this long and painful bit between the start and the finish when we are right in the middle of the open lake. We are swimming and struggling, but no matter how hard we try, nothing seems to be moving. The trees behind us do not get smaller, and the shore in front of us does not seem to get nearer. This is where a lot of people give up. This is the moment where we really need the grit to keep on swimming.

To put it simply: If we want to achieve our goals, we need grit.

Beware of tunnel view and stupid grit

Is there any downside to being gritty? Can we be too gritty?

Well, grit can lead to quite the opposite of living a comfortable life. Always striving and working towards excellence can be exhausting, and there are other pitfalls.

We have to be aware of the so-called "tunnel view." That means that when we are gritty, we can be focused so much on one particular goal that we might overlook better options.

We might also be more vulnerable to the so-called "sunk-cost fallacy," meaning we keep trying to achieve something even though we would do better to give up on it. Think of the businessman who keeps on throwing money at a bad investment because he desperately wants to make it successful. Think of the athlete who misses the right time to retire and ruins his body by being in the game for too long. Think of the casino visitor who keeps on betting money because he wants to win his losses back.

So, there is such a thing as "stupid grit." And let's be honest, all of us have been there: in a toxic relationship we desperately tried to turn around against the advice of our friends, or in a job we hated and knew we should leave. Thus, we should pause at times and ask ourselves if we are on the right track.

But, handled correctly, grit is a very positive– and often heroic– trait to possess.

Purpose, Practice, Positivity – how to learn grit

The good news is that grit is not a God-given trait. We can learn to become grittier.

One way to find our grit is to find our true passion. The hard work we put in feels more manageable if we know it helps us to reach a meaningful goal. Following a clear purpose often prevents us from going in the wrong direction.

Practice is another pivotal part of becoming grittier. We can build in moments of deliberate practice, which will push us out of our comfort zone and stretch our limits.

Think about it: When we see people doing extraordinary things, we do not question how they got there. We tell ourselves, "Well, they are geniuses, prodigies, born with a talent to do those things. I could never do those things."

But ultimately, it was just a series of mundane tasks that they learned and practiced over and over again with sheer persistence until they finally created this extraordinary outcome. If we see someone who has achieved greatness, there will be a long journey and a life story filled with hardships behind them.

Given time, dedication, and practice, we can all achieve great things. After all, success isn't as sweet and rewarding if it has been too easy.

Grit is not only critical to success, but, luckily, it is also pretty straightforward. What's hard about it is being able to stay positive over time.

It's difficult to stay positive when we battle various challenges in our lives. But we can do ourselves a favor and not give up if we think the effort will be worth it. We can remind ourselves of the end goal.

Until we've tried everything, we cannot let negativity take over. It is often darkest before dawn. The obstacles are usually the highest right before the breakthrough. Stay persistent because the tipping point and success might be around the next corner. And if not after the next turn, it will be after the next or after the next. Hang in there. There is an answer to everything.

And do hang out with gritty people. Other people influence our behavior more than we think.

Gritty heroes

Let's take a look at heroes and their grit.

As a starter, think of all the protagonists in sports movies. They do not always win, but they have one thing in common: They do not give up.

We come back to Rocky Balboa, the quintessential archetype of all sports movie heroes. As Rocky eloquently puts it: "Life is not about how hard of a hit we can give. It is about how many we can take and still keep moving forward."

Rocky is a nobody but gets chosen to fight the current world heavyweight champion. Others would have been frozen by anxiety and just quit. If Rocky taught us anything, it was to keep fighting no matter what. The reward was becoming the world heavyweight champion and the greatest fictional boxer ever to appear on a movie screen.

We don't have to be the smartest, tallest, strongest, or wisest to save the earth. Staying in the game is often more crucial for achieving our goals than our talent and abilities.

Remember Samwise Gamgee in LORD OF THE RINGS? He was Frodo's most faithful friend and companion. Sam travelled with Frodo for thousands of miles on foot through Middle-earth and up to the top of Mount Doom and was crucial in conquering a great evil.

Did good old Samwise score high in any virtues that people superficially associate with prodigies or talented people? Was he stronger, smarter, or better looking than others? Hell, no. He drank and swore too often, and he had awfully hairy feet and was clearly overweight. But there was one thing that distinguished him from others: his resilience, his unwillingness to quit. His grit.

When Frodo loses the strength to climb Mount Doom, Sam picks Frodo up and carries him the last few steps. In reality, Frodo never would have completed his quest had Sam not stuck by his side every step of the way. And that ultimately made Sam a hero in his own right.

Think of an even more extreme example: FORREST GUMP. He is born mentally disabled and, on top of that, suffers from a walking disability. But Forrest overcomes all his limitations through stubborn perseverance, and he keeps on going no matter what, standing tall against whatever life throws at him. In the end, he saves eight lives in war; becomes a millionaire, a father, and a loving husband; and is responsible for the success of Elvis Presley and the dude who paints smiley faces on t-shirts.

Pretty impressive, right?

Han Solo is another hero with grit. He is betrayed by one of his best friends, kidnapped by an unscrupulous bounty hunter, frozen in carbonite, and just plain knocked down over and over again. But he always gets up, and then he helps to destroy the Death Star. In the end, he even gets the princess. Try to stop this guy. You can' t. That' s true grit.

It doesn't have to be physical grit to achieve something great. Think of ERIN BROCKOVICH or every single James Stewart character. They fought against gigantic, evil systems. No matter what hardship they had to go through, they just refused to give up and eventually beat the system.

It is the big scenes we remember

Life is short. We must set the compass towards our passion and do something we can be thoroughly proud of. Achieving greatness takes time. Sometimes a whole life. Rome wasn't built in one day, either.

It is the big scenes in movies we remember. Our mission in life should be to create those big scenes that we will never forget; and be recognized for. If we give up on the way, there is only a little chance that we will experience those big moments.

Listen to Will Smith's words: "You might have more talent than me, you might be smarter than me, you might be sexier than me, you might be all of those things — you got it on me in nine categories. But if we get on the treadmill together, there are two things: You're getting off first, or I'm going to die. It's really that simple."

Here's a simpler version by James Bond himself: "I don't stop when I'm tired. I stop when I'm done."

Hang in there. Have grit. Heroes do. It is worth it.

FOR THE IMPATIENT AND HURRIED

Three ways to develop more grit:

1. GIVE IT MEANING

Once we give the task, we do a sense or a purpose, it becomes much easier to hang in there and be persistent.

2. TRUST OUR ABILITIES

If there's a setback (and there will be,) we don't tell ourselves that we don't have what it takes. Instead, we keep in mind that we are ever-evolving creatures and capable of learning. We trust our abilities and practice so we can do it better next time.

3. HANG OUT WITH GRITTY PEOPLE

We are inevitably influenced by people around us. Choose the gritty ones to work with, and their grit will rub off on us.

4 POSITIVITY

...or why attitude defines the outcome

Imagine a young businessman who is sentenced to two consecutive life terms in prison for the alleged murder of his wife and her lover– a crime he never committed. He has to do time in a horrible jail with inhuman conditions and sadistic prison wardens who enjoy torturing the inmates. If that wasn't bad enough, the prison is, of course, also packed with brutal criminals who abuse him.

However, our businessman manages to slowly build positive relationships with some of the inmates as well as with the prison wardens. Even more important, he stays mentally intact, and after nineteen long years, he finally manages to escape from this torture to start a new life in freedom.

This is the story of Andy Dufresne in the film THE SHAWSHANK REDEMPTION.

What kept Andy alive and sane over all those years? His positivity. He stayed positive and optimistic, no matter how bleak the situation was. His positivity proved to be infectious and not only helped him and his fellow inmates to remain mentally intact. He sent a strong message: While the body may be locked away in a cell, the spirit can never be imprisoned.

Heroes are positive

In a 2010 psychological study, researchers from the University of British Columbia found that people identified as heroes were more likely to put a positive spin on adverse events. (9) Heroes are positive thinkers by nature, which contributes to their ability to look past the immediate danger of a situation and see a more optimistic outcome.

Heroes know that even in the darkest moments, there are positive turns ahead. Somewhere. Disaster can be a gift. If events don't go to plan, we can't change the events, but we can change the plan.

But what does positivity mean? Well, in its purest form, it is the practice of being positive or optimistic in attitude. People with high positivity and optimism react to issues with a sense of confidence and with the belief that negative incidents are temporary and manageable.

Positivity predicts a longer life

Let's take a look at the advantages of staying positive and optimistic.

Countless studies in the field of positive psychology suggest that being positive is both mentally and physically healthy. (10) The sheer act of being more positive and optimistic can not only boost our immune system but also help prevent chronic disease. It can even predict a longer life.

Optimism may, indeed, be one of the most important predictors of mental health. Since optimists experience less distress through their positive attitude, they are less prone to suffer from anxiety disorders and depression.

As opposed to pessimists, people with a positive attitude are less likely to be in denial and do not distance themselves from a problem. Instead, they actively tackle issues and accept the situation's reality. Optimists not only have a coping advantage over pessimists; they also have a better chance of learning from difficulties and mistakes. That's because optimists acknowledge and face those difficulties rather than ignoring them.

Furthermore, having a sunny disposition can have a profound impact on our romantic life. In a 2006 study by the American Psychological Association, researchers found that people with a positive attitude are not only perceived as more attractive but tend to be happier in their relationships. (11) And it doesn't matter if both partners are optimists or only one.

The lesson here is: if we cannot be an optimist no matter how hard we try, we should at least date one. It will do our love lives good!

So, as we have seen, positivity can have profound effects not only on our mental health but also on our physical health.

Don't be the fool on the hill

Are there any downsides to being positive? Can we be *too* positive?

Here are some words of caution: optimists tend to underestimate risks, which can be undesirable in moments of imminent physical danger. Just think of the fool who is joyfully walking towards the cliff with his head in the air. He never expects to be falling anytime soon. Optimists are also less critical of deceitful strangers and thus more prone to be cheated.

Research suggests that overly optimistic people are not well prepared for adverse life events and setbacks, as such things don't fit their world view. When there is a significant mismatch between our beliefs and the outcome, we get frustrated and disappointed. (12)

The problem with too much positive thinking is that we might only visualize the glorious moment of victory: receiving an Academy Award on stage, crossing the finish line after our first

Olympic Games, or marrying the movie star we are secretly in love with. But mentally achieving the goal has, of course, nothing to do with actually achieving it.

A better way is to not only dream about that success as an end goal, but also to envision all the obstacles and hurdles that are in the way and how we can overcome them– with a positive mindset, of course.

To conclude: it is definitely advantageous to be guided by a positive outlook. However, it is even better to curb our sunny dispositions at times with a small dose of realism to prevent us from taking unnecessary risks or acting recklessly.

The key is to be balanced. We should celebrate our positivity but be optimistically realistic!

Positivity can be learned

The remaining question is: Are we born as either optimists or pessimists? There is an ongoing nature vs. nurture debate, and yes, some people are indeed born more optimistic than others. However, there is a strong case that positive thinking and optimism can be learned.

One step to being more positive– though as a fiction writer and daydreamer, I hate to say this– is to separate fact from fiction. Most of our negative thoughts are, well, just thoughts and have little to do with reality.

Next time we ruminate on negative feelings, we should combat them with a quick fact check: Is there really no way out? Is the situation unchangeable and hopeless? Will this setback last forever? The answer to all of those questions is almost always a definite *no*. Negative thought rarely survive the clash with reality. Strangely enough, reality is our best ally against pessimism.

Another remedy against too much negativity is living a life with a clear purpose. Setbacks are just minor bumps on the long journey towards fulfilling our life mission if we live with purpose.

If we remember the *why* of our lives, adverse events will drown in a sea of unimportance. (We will take a closer look at that in the chapter about purpose)

If things look bleak, another quick fix is to focus on one positive element. If there seems to be nothing positive in the present moment, there is always something from the past that can lift us up. Any positive thought can refocus the brain's attention to the good. As Professor Dumbledore said in HARRY POTTER AND THE PRISONER OF AZKABAN: "Happiness can be found, even in the darkest of times, if one only remembers to turn on the light."

Showing gratitude is another essential element on the way to being more positive. There has been much academic research on the advantages of being grateful and why it helps positivity. Grateful people have been found to be more positive, to have a greater sense of belonging, and experience fewer episodes of depression and stress. (13)

It is good to stand still at times and remind ourselves of the beauty all around us in our lives. We can start a gratitude journal and write on a daily basis about things we feel grateful for. Writing down these good memories helps to capture them and prevent them from being forgotten in less optimistic times.

And, yes, it's best to stay away from negative people who drag us down. Better to enjoy, and be inspired by, the company of people who display a positive mindset.

Especially ignore naysayers! They are prepared to say no to everything. Always remember how Emperor Joseph II rejected one of the biggest musical geniuses of all time, Wolfgang Amadeus Mozart: "Too many notes, Mozart, and too beautiful for our ears."

In story terms, naysayers are called "threshold guardians" or "gatekeepers." These are the people who decide whether or not we will make it over the next hurdle. They are the publisher to whom we send our book proposal, the casting agent for whom we audition, or the Human Resources officer who receives our CV.

Most often, they are negative. They *will* say no. Often, they are *instructed* to say no. They are *conditioned* to say no. They will say no and no and no. Sometimes this is because they envy those who are successful and try to discourage them.

But we must accept these gatekeepers as an integral part of our stories and life journeys. The hidden beauty of these threshold guardians is that they often create an internal discomfort and challenge us to find a new way of thinking or acting. They are there to test our worthiness and commitment to get to our next desired stage, and they provide the necessary resistance to build the new skills we need to continue the journey.

Naysayers can redirect us to another, better path for the journey. We might have a straight way planned out, but then the gatekeepers reject us and send us on an unplanned detour. In hindsight, this often turns out to be a better path.

So, stay positive and bless all the naysayers and rejecters along the way. They most likely do us a favor when they reject us.

Heroes have a shot at a silver lining

All heroes are positive.

Well, almost all of them. Admittedly, there are those Woody Allen -type anti-heroes who are somewhat skeptical and cynical about life in general. They always expect the worst and feel guilty when they are in good spirits once in a while. But there is a reason why they are called anti-heroes, and it's because they often serve as a reminder of how *not* to approach life.

In general, heroes tackle their adventures with a great deal of positivity. Would Andy Dufresne in THE SHAWSHANK REDEMPTION have survived nineteen years of unjustified imprisonment without a positive outlook? No.

Heroes know that there is always something good out there. There is still a way out. No situation, no matter how difficult it is, is hopeless.

As Andy Dufresne says: "I guess it comes down to a simple choice. Get busy living or get busy dying."

The movie SILVER LININGS PLAYBOOK is based on the premise that positivity can literally save our lives. Its hero, Pat Solitano, comes back from a severe mental breakdown that almost drove him to suicide. By going out, taking on running, and trying to be optimistic about his circumstances, he slowly gets out of his misery.

At one point, he says to his state-appointed therapist, "I hate my illness. I want to control it. This is what I believe to be true: We have to do everything we can, and if we stay positive we have a shot at a silver lining."

As a reward for staying positive, he eventually gets both mental sanity and his love interest, Tiffany, in the end.

DALLAS BUYERS CLUB is the true story of rodeo rider Ron Woodroof, one of the first people known to be infected with HIV. Instead of dwelling on all the negative aspects and waiting for the virus to slowly kill him, he starts fighting for a good cause. He instigates campaigns for humane medical treatment for HIV patients and forms a club to smuggle the medicine to those in need. By doing so, he helps thousands of others to live longer and healthier lives. Ron eventually dies of the disease in 1992, a whole seven years later than his doctors predicted.

Attitude defines the outcome

Next time we encounter a problematic situation, think of Winston Churchill's famous words: "A pessimist sees the difficulty in every opportunity; an optimist sees the opportunity in every difficulty." We can decide which one we want to be.

The German philosopher Arthur Schopenhauer once said that the quality of life is determined by how we interpret our experience, not by the experience itself. True words.

We always have the choice to be positive or negative in any situation. No darkness continues forever. Every tunnel has a light at the end, even if we don't see it yet.

The last lesson comes from the great Henry Ford. "Whether you think you can, or you think you can't...either way, you are right."

Attitude often defines the outcome. Think positive, and there is a higher likelihood that the results will be positive, too. That's what heroes do.

FOR THE IMPATIENT AND HURRIED

Three ways to become more positive:

1. SEPARATE FACT FROM FICTION

Most negative thoughts do not survive the clash with reality. Instead of dwelling on negativity, we can make a little reality check and see that things are less gloomy than we thought.

2. FOCUS ON ONE POSITIVE ELEMENT

There is always one positive element in pretty much every mess. We can find it and fixate on it. Often only one little positive thought can refocus the brain's attention to the good.

3. BE GRATEFUL

We can remind ourselves of the beauty on this planet in general and in our lives in particular. Starting a gratitude journal and writing grateful letters to people we care about are perfect places to start.

5 STOICISM

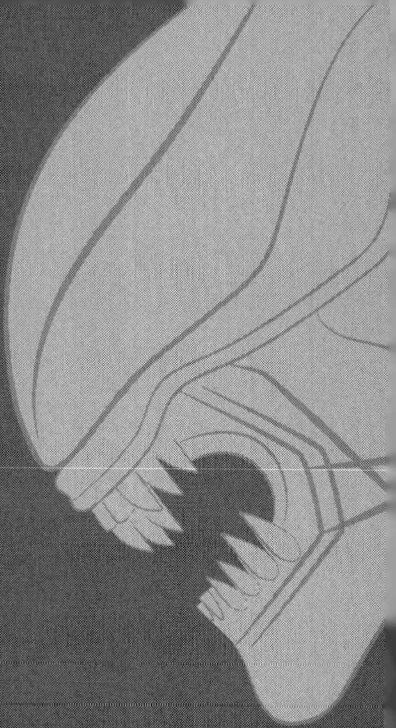

...or why
crises
are nice
little helpers

Consider the following movie outlines.

A macabre space alien that multiplies through transplanting its embryos into human bodies threatens to wipe out humanity, but Ripley arrives on the scene and defeats it.

A villain threatens to destroy the world, but along comes James Bond and kills him before he can do so.

Lord Voldemort threatens to make the whole world his slave, but then Harry Potter comes along and defeats him.

Those outlines sound a little incomplete, right!? That is because one crucial story element is missing: the crisis.

Let's take a look at how the ALIEN storyline would read with a crisis included:

A commercial spaceship with seven crew members in stasis is on a return trip back to Earth. But in the middle of the journey, they are awakened and discover they have a horrifying space alien on board that multiplies through transplanting its embryos into human bodies. One by one, the creature kills all crew members in cruel ways until only Ripley, the courageous warrant officer, is still alive.

After a high-intensity chase, Ripley manages to exit the ship by an escape shuttle. She leaves the mothership to self-destruct, assuming the alien is still on board. But soon after, she is horrified to learn that the alien sneaked onto the escape shuttle with her.

A climactic deadly fight ensues, during which Ripley almost gets killed. In the last effort in which Ripley has to use all her wit and strength, she can finally defeat the creature and blast it out into the depths of space.

Much better now that a moment of crisis is included, right?

The crisis is the moment of highest tension. The audience in the cinema becomes completely silent because this is the moment when the hero is on the verge of being defeated. Simply put: Without a moment of crisis, there is no suspense, no drama, and– ultimately – no story. It is ultimately the crisis that triggers change and shapes the heroic consciousness of the story's protagonist.

Nobody said it would be easy

Crises happen in every good story, and they happen to every single hero out there. At one point on their journey, a crisis hits the hero severely. Often the crisis hits so hard that it looks like all could end tragically– and sometimes it does. The crisis is the pivotal moment in a hero's story. It's the make-or-break moment. Only a deep crisis teaches the hero the right skills to succeed in the final battle against evil forces.

As in every good story, there are crises in every life. They happen. Inevitably. If we try hard to avoid them, we probably won't end up doing anything too interesting.

The higher we aim, and the bigger the adventures we embark on, the more crises there will be. Some will be small. A few will be really big. Some will be purely age-related, with the most prominent of these being the mid-life crisis. Most other crises are purely situational, though some can be existential and very painful. Nobody said it would be easy.

Why astronauts learn stoicism

Now that we know that crises *will* happen, we need to know how to react to them. The good news is that there is one thing that is always and entirely in our control: ourselves.

Think about it. What is worse? A) Being in a very difficult situation or B) Being in a very difficult situation ***and*** in a mental state of despair. To restate: Difficult moments and crises will happen, but the way we react to them is, to a large extent, our choice.

The issue with crisis situations is that people tend to make ill-fated judgements and take actions they wouldn't under normal circumstances. Research shows that the emotional states of anxiety, worry, and anger that generally happen in a crisis harm our decision-making process. Worrying reduces thinking power, and negative emotions often drive us to premature closure. (14) Not good.

This is why martial arts professionals focus as much on mental training as they do on physical training. This is why astronauts are extensively trained to stay calm in crisis situations. Neither of these groups can afford to panic in a difficult situation. Every mistake could be fatal.

So how do heroes handle those stressful, anxiety-laden crisis situations? The answer is: very stoically.

Stoicism is an ancient school of philosophy that has been with us for more than two thousand years. One of the key teachings in stoicism is about keeping self-control and objectivity in critical situations. Stoicism teaches us to emotionally detach from any situation and change perception so that the only consideration given is to hard facts.

This does not mean we should completely eliminate our emotions before making any decisions. It means trying to eliminate those emotions which blur our decision-making: the ones which lead to anger, rage, or apathy. With a clear and unbiased view, we can make rational decisions even in times of the biggest adversity.

How to foster stoicism

The good news is that we can learn to be more stoic.

Next time we face a crisis, remember that any decision driven by anxiety and made in the heat of the moment will be a flawed one. In those moments, we must try to control our own emotions and nerves; and we should definitely ignore the panic of others. Often, we cannot control external events, but we can control ourselves. If possible, we should delay a decision until things cool down.

Another way to defeat a crisis is with logic. We can be calm about the things we cannot change and only focus on the ones which are under our control. Can anyone be physically harmed or die from what is happening? If the answer is no, the situation is not all that bad, and there are most likely ways to overcome the crisis.

We should even go a step further and regard the crisis as a gift. The English word "crisis" is derived from the ancient Greek word *krisis*, which means a "vitally important or decisive state of things; a point at which change must come, for better or worse."

The emphasis should be on 'change'; and crises are always about change. They are indeed a perfect opportunity to act on things we have long put on the back burner. Use them for drastic and, sometimes, long-overdue changes - changes we might not make under normal circumstances. In a crisis, we have nothing to lose.

Don't let a crisis go to waste. Try to see an opportunity in every crisis.

Of Mr. Spock and other stoic heroes

Think of some stoic heroes from film history.

Yoda, the little green Jedi master from STAR WARS, is a prime example of stoicism. Even when the galaxy is on the brink of destruction and the attacks of the Empire are getting more severe and more frequent, he resists personal revenge and makes wise and analytical decisions. And he helps the good forces to succeed in the end.

This gets mirrored in STAR TREK with Mr. Spock, who remains stoic no matter how imminent the danger may be. By keeping his cool, he balances well with Captain Kirk, who sometimes acts rather impulsively.

Think of the third instalment of the Indiana Jones series: INDIANA JONES AND THE LAST CRUSADE. The story centers around Indy's frantic search for the Holy Grail and his complicated relationship with his father, an eccentric but stoic character. In the climactic finale, his father sees his son, Indiana, desperately trying to reach the Holy Grail in a collapsing temple, which is about to kill them all. Indy's father stays calm and convinces his son to let go of the grail. By doing so, he saves his son's life.

Think of other stoic heroes, like Agatha Christie's master detectives Miss Marple and Hercule Poirot. Those characters never lose their clarity of thought, no matter how tense the situation.

Think of the human rights lawyer Atticus Finch in TO KILL A MOCKINGBIRD, who kept his head up and his mind clear when confronted with a mob driven by hate and racism.

Think of Gromit from WALLACE & GROMIT. Whereas Wallace often panics and loses his head during their frenzied adventures, his dog Gromit keeps a cool head and brings things stoically to an end.

Take Clint Eastwood, the lonesome and laconic cowboy in Sergio Leone's *Dollar* trilogy. He keeps his cool no matter what happens, and he is the one in THE GOOD, THE BAD AND THE UGLY who succeeds and gets the treasure. Since he is not driven by pure revenge like his opponent Tuco, or by evil greed like the villain Angel Eyes, he gets neither shot nor left tied up on a remote desert grave. Instead, he rides into the sunset with the gold chest.

Often in their moment of crisis, heroes find that what they want has become inconsistent with their value system. They must now make a tough decision that goes against their life dreams. But it is only through the crisis and the tough choices that come with it that these heroes find their true selves.

That is what happens to the protagonist of the movie TOOTSIE; an unemployed actor named Michael disguises himself as a woman in a desperate effort to have the movie career he has always dreamed of. But Michael reaches a point where he must choose between what he always wanted– being a movie star– and what he really needs– his great love, Julie. He can't have both and has to make a tough crisis decision.

In a moment of clarity, Michael gives up on his movie career, exposes himself as a cheat, and chooses Julie, even though he doesn't even know if she will ever return his feelings. An uncertain outcome never hinders a hero from making the right decision.

Crises are nice little helpers

One truly stoic hero from real life was the 19th-century American president, Abraham Lincoln. His life seems to have been in one continuous crisis, but he was able to succeed with the aid of his calmness and stoicism in moments of greatest despair.

Born into poverty in a one-room log cabin somewhere in Kentucky, Abe Lincoln lost his mother and was forced out of his home when he was still a boy. He went bankrupt in his early twenties when his business partner and best friend died. He was engaged to be married to his teenage sweetheart, but she died before the wedding. Then, at the age of 27, he had such a severe nervous breakdown that he had to stay in bed for six months with a major depression.

However, Abe did get up, and stoically continued his journey. There were many more setbacks, failures, and crises in his life, but eventually, Abraham Lincoln became the president of the

United States and led his country through its greatest constitutional, military, and moral crisis: the American Civil War. In the end, he preserved the Union, abolished slavery, and modernized the economy.

A private soldier's diary entry about Lincoln's appearance illustrates Abe's strength and stoicism through crisis most vividly: "None of us to our dying day can forget that countenance... Concentrated in that one great, strong, yet tender face, the agony of the life and death struggle of the hour was revealed as we had never seen it before. With a new understanding, we knew why we were soldiers."

If a colleague constantly moans about traffic jams during rush hour or broken coffee machines, tell him Lincoln's story. That might bring his problems into perspective.

Go out there and stoically greet those obstacles with optimism and pragmatism. Be aware that they will only be little bumps on the long way to fulfil our vision. Life is a marathon, not a sprint, so we cannot waste all our energy on this one crisis.

Stoicism is especially handy when we are in a leadership position. If we don't keep our calm when the shit hits the fan... who will!?

Crises can be even nice little helpers, as they not only test our resilience but also show us how not to do something. They can lead us to new and unexpected ways on our exciting journey called life.

We can either get bitter or we can get better. Choose to get better. Be stoic and grateful the next time you encounter a crisis.

Think about it. If we only take advantage of the easy opportunities that arise in life, we might fall short of getting where we really want to be. We must also take advantage of adversities and turn them into positives.

Think of Salman Rushdie's words: "How do we defeat terrorism? Don't be terrorized." Heroes face their terror with utmost stoicism. And so, should we.

FOR THE IMPATIENT AND HURRIED

Three steps to deal with crises:

1. EMOTIONAL DETACHMENT

Ignore panic. Ignore emotions. Focus only on what can be controlled. If possible, do not make important decisions in the heat of the moment.

2. APPLY LOGIC

Analyze carefully whether the consequences are really all that bad or if they are just momentarily blown out of proportion. If no physical harm can happen, it usually is not all that bad.

3. DON'T LET CRISES GO TO WASTE

Crises are good opportunities to undertake drastic and long-overdue changes. Take advantage of crises; they can be effective catalysts for change.

PART II

SUPER-EGO

the critical moralizer

6 INTEGRITY

...or why heroes don't expect an audience

Imagine a single mother of three who lives in Southern California, barely making enough money to feed her kids or herself. She is desperate for a job. Eventually, she finds a seemingly insignificant job as a legal assistant in a California law firm, which pays her just enough money to get by.

On her first day, she is appointed to look through some paperwork on a small real estate case. By chance, she finds evidence that the huge corporation known as the Pacific Gas and Electric Company (PG&E) could have contaminated the groundwater in the small town of Hinkley.

Against both her job description and her boss's orders, she digs deeper into that case. She finds that the people of Hinkley have indeed been severely medically damaged by the contamination.

After several days away from the office doing this research, she is fired by her boss because he believes she was neglecting her job. However, she makes a passionate plea to her boss that this case is worth pursuing, and he reluctantly takes her back.

She must make great sacrifices in her life as the legal costs mount, and the round-the-clock work leaves her out of touch with both her boyfriend and her kids. At one point, she even gets chased down and physically threatened by PG&E and their henchmen.

But she continues with her case. She defies all odds and almost single-handedly brings down the seemingly invincible corporation, making them pay a settlement amount of $333 million to the harmed townspeople.

The heroine of this story is called ERIN BROCKOVICH in the eponymous Academy-Award-winning movie, based on true events.

Ethical challenges can be complex

The story of Erin Brockovich illustrates another essential point about heroes: They have an intact moral compass and strong personal integrity. Those virtues guide heroes through hard times and support their decisions, even if it means taking a personal risk.

What is a moral compass? It is ultimately our inner guide for decision-making based on our morals and virtues. The moral compass helps us to decide what is right and wrong in every situation.

The ethical challenges we face on our journeys can be complex. We never know in advance when something will happen to challenge our moral integrity. But if such a thing happens and our integrity is tested, we need to have a strong ethical foundation and moral instincts we can rely on.

It isn't hard to make right decisions in good times. When things are going smooth and in the right direction, it is easy to make an honorable decision.

Our decision-making process comes under pressure though, when we are faced with risk, danger, or uncertainty of any kind–when the so-called shit hits the fan (and on a Hero's Journey it *will* hit the fan sooner or later.) It is significantly harder to make a moral decision when we are under enormous pressure and have to act quickly.

During a crisis, we will be challenged when we least expect it. If we do not have a healthy moral compass, we may end up making a decision that does not comply with our values.

Integrity holds our virtues together

The important character trait that decides the direction of the moral compass is integrity.

Integrity is the quality of being honest, trustworthy, and fair. It implies having strong moral principles. The word integrity is derived from the Latin word for "wholeness" and thus implies the state of being complete, undivided, intact, and unbroken. Integrity is the glue that holds our virtues together. As German social psychologist, Erich Fromm put it, "Integrity simply means a willingness not to violate one's identity."

Why is integrity so crucial for our lives?

To start with, it is much easier for a person to follow their sense of integrity than to override it. Making unethical decisions might be easier and more comfortable in the short term, but our wrongdoings eventually come back like a boomerang. Life is empty and stressful when we always have to remember our lies, if we have to live with the anxiety of getting caught, or if we do not feel we truly earned our reward because we cheated our way up.

Even more important: If we stay true to our moral compass and integrity, we can be ourselves no matter what situation we find ourselves in.

A simple example: We have all met people in our lives who behave like chameleons. They are different people depending on their social environment. They are different with us, at home, at work, and in their social clubs. They act as alternate personas depending on their environment. They live their lives as multiple characters, depending on what they think each social group wants them to be. But that is terribly stressful, and they usually end up feeling fragmented and confused as to who they really are.

Think about it: No relationship, whether private or professional, should require that we pretend to be a character we are not. If people don't like who we really are, why would we want to be involved with them in the first place?

A person of integrity is a person others can count on. People know he will do what he says. His friends feel comfortable opening up to him and turning to him in times of crisis. Is there anything better than being needed and respected by friends?

Being a person of integrity has other positive impacts. Research in the field of positive psychology, spearheaded by psychologist and educator Martin Seligman, showed that a strong perception of meaning and integrity leads to significantly better mental well-being and physical health. (15)

Fostering integrity

So how exactly are we going to live a life with more integrity? Well, it is always a good start for us to look inside and decide who we want to be– and then be that person. Say what we mean. Do what we say we will do. Don't take credit for the success of others. Remember the action bit: Don't just talk the talk, walk the walk!

Most important, we should always think of the effects our actions have on others. If guided by an intact moral compass, our actions should express the way that we ourselves would like to be treated.

A simple integrity test is to ask ourselves: *If my motives and actions were made 100% visible for all to see, would I be able to stand behind them? Would I be proud of them?*

Think about the opposite of a hero for a moment. Think about people who act without integrity. Think of Bernie Madoff. Think of the Enron bosses who manipulated financial accounts and established fraudulent schemes for their own financial benefit.

These might have been decent people at the beginning of their life journeys, but they were lured by power and money and got corrupted along their way. Quick monetary success and the pleasure that comes with it destroyed any ethical beliefs they might have had beforehand. On their greedy journey, they not only destroyed their own lives but the lives of many others. Their moral compass was broken.

What Rick and Cool Hand Luke have in common

All heroes follow a strong moral compass and act with integrity. If they are not doing so at the beginning of their journey, they definitely do so by the end. Otherwise, they wouldn't be heroes.

Think of ERIN BROCKOVICH again. As an unemployed single mother, she had a hard time surviving and feeding her children properly. But Brockovich resisted short-term success and even faced an imminent threat to her own life by doing what she thought was right: Suing a big corporation that had acted inhumanely, thereby trying to help everyone who had fallen victim to it. She followed her ethical beliefs, acted true to her integrity, and was ready to sacrifice her own life for the cause.

Think of Rick, the main character in the classic movie CASABLANCA. Rick is the stranded bar owner in Casablanca during WWII. He is bitter over losing the love of his life, Ilsa, and drowns his sorrows with booze and cynicism. One day Ilsa returns and gives him a second chance for a relationship, something he has always yearned for.

But at the end of this classic film, Rick lets her go. Why? Because he knew that he could not have made her happy. Even more important, she has a bigger role to play in life: fighting the Nazis. Rick stayed true to his integrity by rejecting personal success and short-term pleasure, and this was ultimately better for everybody involved. It was a tough decision, but Rick rediscovered his moral compass just in time.

Think about Paul Newman in COOL HAND LUKE. He rebels against the inhumane conditions in the prison where he is doing time. The sadistic guards put him in solitary confinement; they make him do unbearable physical work; they torture and beat him, but they cannot destroy his integrity.

In the end, when the prison guards realize he will never break, they shoot him. Cool Hand Luke's integrity was too strong for them. But he didn't die for nothing; his heroic deeds ultimately helped his fellow inmates to make better decisions about their own lives.

Heroes do the right thing, even when they don't know if it will pay off in the end. For them, it is better to die standing up than live a life on their knees.

Often heroes start out as rather questionable characters and only find their integer self later on their long journey. The Clint Eastwood movie GRAN TORINO is the redemption story of the intolerant, selfish, and slightly racist Walt Kowalski. In the movie's climactic scene, Walt walks into a death trap to help an Asian immigrant family he has come to love and admire. He has made it is his purpose to protect and help them.

A young priest, who knows about the imminent danger, pleads with him to leave in peace and escape the trap. But Walt walks into his probable death saying, "I am at peace." Paying the ultimate price by sacrificing oneself is an integral part of Walt's journey, and many other Hero's Journeys.

It doesn't have to be always that dramatic. But one remarkable characteristic of heroes is that they do not do good for the sake of doing good. Character is what we are when no one is watching. Heroes don't expect an audience or a reward for their good deeds. They stay true to their moral compass and integrity, no matter what the situation.

Billy Wilder's fabulous movie THE APARTMENT is the bittersweet story of an inconspicuous man named CC Baxter, who works as an insurance clerk somewhere in a soulless, open-plan office in New York City. In hopes of getting a faster climb up the corporate ladder, CC lets his senior co-workers use his apartment for their various extramarital affairs.

The extramarital encounters of his co-workers turn out to be rather noisy, leading CC's neighbors to assume he is a playboy who brings home another woman every night. That is quite ironic because CC is actually shy around the opposite sex and no womanizer at all.

Eventually CC's plan seems to work, and he gets the promotion he always dreamed of. But when he realizes that he cannot conform to his boss's unethical practices anymore, he refuses the promotion, quits his job, and is ready to leave everything behind. He has to decide between success and integrity. He chooses integrity and finally decides to become a "mensch."

He does so without telling anybody– not even his love interest, Miss Kubelik, who would surely have been impressed by his ethical actions.

CC Baxter and other heroes do not need the big stage to do good. They do not need praise or glory. They do good because it is their deeply held belief that they should do good, and they follow this belief.

Value integrity more than success

Exactly that is demonstrated by the true and moving story of an actual twentieth-century hero: Irena Sendler.

Irena Sendler was an ordinary Catholic woman from Poland who saved almost 2,500 Jewish children from the Holocaust. She risked her life by issuing false identity papers to help Jewish children escape the Warsaw Ghetto and then placing these children with families all over Poland. She kept careful track of the children's true identities, hoping that someday after the war, she could return them to their original families.

Sadly, the Nazis discovered Sendler's activities in 1943. They captured her and tortured her by breaking her feet and legs. But Irena bravely refused to betray any of her friends or the children she had sent away to safety.

Irena Sendler managed to escape the Nazis and lived in obscurity after the war. When asked about her heroic deeds many years later, she wrote: "Every child saved with my help is the justification of my existence on this Earth and not a title to glory." She never claimed any credit for her actions and only said, "Heroes do extraordinary things. What I did wasn't extraordinary. It was normal."

Her heroic deeds only became known to a wider audience in the year 2000, when a group of high school students from Kansas discovered her story and turned it into a play. Irena Sendler died in 2008 at the age of 98, just one year after she was nominated for the Nobel Peace Prize. Bless her.

Just like Irena Sendler, heroes would never hurt their integrity for success. Success is short-term pleasure, while integrity is long-term peace with oneself.

Many heroes may have conflicted minds and troubled personalities, but their moral compass and integrity always remain intact.

"Integrity is the light that guides your way", said the Greek philosopher Plato.

True words. A strong moral compass and integrity show us the way in dark times, and they are the catalyst for long-term happiness. Embrace them. Heroes do.

FOR THE IMPATIENT AND HURRIED

Three steps for living with more integrity:

1. ACT ON THE CATEGORICAL IMPERATIVE

This term was coined by the German philosopher Immanuel Kant and is also known as the "Kant Act." It states, "Only act according to that maxim, that it should become a universal law." In other words: Always treat others the same way we would want to be treated.

2. DO WHAT IS RIGHT AND LET THE CONSEQUENCES FOLLOW

We must always do what we think complies with our moral compass and ethical beliefs and not think of the consequences too much. It is better to lose than to lose our integrity.

3. APPLY TRANSPARENCY

If our motives and actions were made 100% visible for everybody to see, could we still stand behind them and be proud of them? Act accordingly.

7 PURPOSEFULNESS

...or why we should be a flying arrow

George Bailey is an ambitious young man born and bred in the small New York town of Bedford Falls. He wants to escape his small hometown and go out and travel the world to do something "big and important."

But every time George saves enough money to embark on this journey, misfortunes get in his way and keep him in his hometown; he has to help his father's business, or do a friend a favor, or spend his savings on a family emergency.

A few years later, he still has not embarked on his desired world trip. Instead, George has settled down with his family and runs his father's business. He leads exactly the "ordinary" life he always tried to escape.

At this point, George Bailey comes to believe that he has completely failed and is contemplating suicide. His life did not go the way he planned. He got stuck in his small hometown and never achieved something "big and important" as he had always desired. In a moment of darkness and despair, he is on the verge of jumping off a bridge.

Before he can take his own life, the second-class angel Clarence Odbody appears and proves to George that his life was the complete opposite of a failure. He presents to George the vision of a dystopian future world in which George Bailey never existed. In this parallel universe, all of his friends are worse off, the town was taken over by a villain, and his wife ended up a bitter and lonely maid.

Once confronted with a world in which he never existed, George finally realizes what his purpose is: not doing "great things" but many small things in a great way. He concludes that he made all the villagers around him happier and better people by acting helpfully and courageously towards them each day. Now that he understands his purpose and realizes his existence does have meaning, he can fully appreciate his life and be happy.

This is the story of Frank Capra's classic IT'S A WONDERFUL LIFE.

A purpose creates focus and clarity

George Bailey and other heroes go through their adventures with all they have. They do not give up and are always on a trajectory to fulfil their mission, even if it means risking their own lives.

Why? Because they are following a strong purpose. Others may refer to this as a "calling" or the "meaning of life." No matter what the name, it is a goal that is larger than oneself. It gives our lives direction and provides us with a sense that we are on this planet for a reason.

All heroes believe in something. Their journey has a strong sense of purpose. They may not have a purpose at the beginning of their journey, but they do at the end. It is their purpose, their belief in a greater goal, that makes them get up in the morning and expose themselves to risks and adventures that could cost them their life. In a pure Hero's Journey, the purpose is apparent in every single scene.

Though we might not have a purpose in every little episode of our lives, we should give our overall lives a purpose. Without a purpose, setbacks can make us feel that the quest is hopeless. But with a purpose, we recognize that obstacles and challenges are a natural part of the journey to fulfil that purpose– and we keep going.

A purpose also helps us get our priorities straight. Our lives become less muddled, less complicated, and less stressful. We have a filter that decides what is important and what is not. We are like an arrow flying towards its target, focused and strong as our purposeful goal remains in sight.

A purpose is mostly external, whether it's helping to improve literacy in developing countries or simply making someone else's day-to-day life a bit more endurable through subtle acts of kindness. A purpose makes us look outward, not inward, and so we are less self-centered. Instead, we begin to feel that we are part of something bigger, which is outside ourselves.

When we focus outward, we have less time to contemplate ourselves. This significantly reduces mind chatter which is often a source of anxiety and depression.

Studies by leading academic institutions verify that having a life purpose leads to a longer and healthier life and even makes a person more resistant to mental illnesses. One particular study by researchers from the University of California at Los Angeles (UCLA) and the University of North Carolina found that people with a deep sense of purpose and meaning in life showed very favorable gene-expression profiles in their immune cells. (16)

The conclusion seems that If we have a strong purpose in life, as opposed to a purely pleasure-seeking existence, we will automatically take better care of ourselves, our body, and our mind because we have something powerful to live for.

There is a prominent form of psychotherapy called ***logotherapy*** that is based on finding purpose and meaning in life. It was invented by the Austrian psychologist Viktor Frankl and is based on his own experience as an inmate in a Nazi concentration camp. Frankl observed that the Auschwitz prisoners who were most likely to survive were those who felt they still had a vital purpose in their lives. (17)

The tragedy of Gazza

Think of the opposite: not having a purpose. In that case, we have no path to follow, so we try to follow someone else's; but this inauthenticity can harm our soul. Without our own clear path, our true potential might be lost.

Without a purpose, there is nothing to fight for. We end up wandering through life, feeling aimless. That can make us vulnerable to anxiety and boredom. Many end up trying to ease their psychological pain with addictive substances and behaviors. Since we have no other purpose, our only goal becomes the short-term satisfaction of those addictions.

Think of the tragic tale of Paul Gascoigne. Known as "Gazza," he was probably the most gifted English footballer of his day. His whole purpose was playing football– what Americans call "soccer"– and being the best footballer, he could possibly be.

But once Gazza retired from football, he no longer had a purpose. He started drinking and using drugs. He beat his wife, spent some time in jail, and was seen stumbling through hotel lobbies asking strangers if they would buy him a drink. As his former football colleague, Gary Lineker rightly said, "Hopefully, Paul can find some sort of goal. He needs a reason to want to get better."

Of course, not everyone who loses their purpose – or never really finds one at all –ends up like Paul Gascoigne. But without a purpose, our lives will likely feel hollow and pointless.

And don't confuse "having a sense of purpose" with happiness and pleasure.

Happiness is often a fleeting moment. It is what happens on our journey and is situation-based. It comes and goes and is mostly short-term.

Purpose goes much deeper. It gives us a strong sense of direction, a sense of meaning, and a sense of overall fulfilment and integrity.

As Fyodor Dostoyevsky said in his seminal work THE

BROTHERS KARAMAZOV: "The mystery of human existence lies not in just staying alive, but in finding something to live for."

Living a purposeful life is not always easy. Acting on our purpose often means we must do things outside our comfort zone and beyond what we think of as the common norm. In those cases, we must trust both our gut feelings and our heart's desire and stay on the path that seems to be the proper way– even if it leads off of the path of convenience.

Most humans long to believe that our lives have a purpose that reaches beyond our lifespan. This longing drives us to work extra hard and, sometimes, experience true pain. But our sense of purpose guides our actions from the past through the present to the future, giving us the sense that we are on the right track.

People who live their purpose also tend to suffer less from death anxiety. Existential psychiatrist and author Irvin Yalom writes in his book STARING AT THE SUN that if we believe we have honestly pursued what we wanted to do in life, the idea of death comes much easier. (18)

How to find purpose in life

One way to find our individual purpose is through pure honesty, which starts with being our pure, authentic selves. If we do the things we love; surround ourselves with people we truly want to be with; travel to places we genuinely want to see; and follow our true passion, it is almost impossible to *not* live on the purposeful path.

There is a creative exercise that can help us find our purpose. It's done by creating a fictional interview with our older self. Ask her or him what they truly enjoyed doing in their past life and what they valued most highly. Then we can go and do what our future-self enjoyed and valued.

But it's important that we don't force an interest in subjects only because they're said to be important. The subject must appeal to us as individuals. We must look at our own values, at the things that ignite us and set our hearts on fire.

Purpose is often found at the intersection of true values and passion. That is the sweet spot of purpose, the place where many heroic journeys begin.

Purposeful heroes

All heroes have strong purposes to live and die for. If they have to go to hell and back by fighting for their purpose, they will. And they will get deep satisfaction along the way, whether they fail or succeed.

Spartacus's purpose is to free thousands of slaves and gladiators in Rome. Batman's purpose is to eradicate crime in the huge and terrifying Gotham City. James Bond's purpose is nothing less than to serve crown and country and save the world, over and over again.

Now, a purpose does not have to be that grand. Take the wonderful character AMELIE in the French movie of the same name. Amelie is a timid young woman who drifts aimlessly through life until she finds her purpose– and that turns out to be simply bringing the people in her little Parisian neighborhood a bit of happiness during their day-to-day struggles.

Often heroes start their journeys without clear a purpose and only find it on their way. One prominent example is Holly Martins, the protagonist of the seminal thriller THE THIRD MAN. He begins as a cynical drunk who comes to post-war Vienna to accept a job offered by his old school friend Harry Lime.

Once in Vienna, Martins learns that Harry Lime has recently died. His death, however, seems suspicious, so Martins decides to stay in Vienna and investigate on his own dime.

Eventually, he finds out that Harry is indeed still alive but has become a criminal. It was Harry who organized the dilution of black-market penicillin and therefore caused many casualties, including hospitalized children.

Disillusioned at first, Martins wants to leave Vienna and forget about his turncoat friend. But then Martins finds his purpose – defending the weak– and starts believing in integrity and serving the greater good. He is finally ready to betray Harry in order to restore justice, even though he knows it will come at the cost of losing his old friend and the love of his life.

Rick Blaine in CASABLANCA goes through a similar journey. Rick starts his journey as a nihilistic cynic but ends it as an idealist who is willing to give up the love of his life for the greater good.

Getting through this thing

It is striking that a hero's purpose is almost always aligned with serving the greater good, making things better, and, in the best case, improving society as a whole.

As Robert F. Kennedy put it concisely: "The purpose of life is to contribute in some way to making things better."

True words. When we follow our purpose, we must do so in an unconditional way. We cannot be thinking of any rewards or returns on investment. This is truly giving love for its own sake to a partner, or to family, or even to the world at large.

The author Kurt Vonnegut said: "We are here to help each other get through this thing, whatever it is."

Having a purpose is not only good for our personal well-being; it gives us direction and, ultimately, a justification for why we are here. There is no more profound feeling of long-term fulfilment and true happiness than finding our true path, following that path, and knowing that we have made a difference.

That's what heroes do.

FOR THE IMPATIENT AND HURRIED

Three steps to finding purpose:

1. PURE HONESTY

Live authentically, surrounded by people you like and doing what you really want to do. Our purpose is often a nice by-product of living this authentic life.

2. INTERVIEWING ONE'S OLDER SELF

We can conduct a fictional interview with an older, future version of ourselves. Ask what they were most proud of in life and see if our own purpose might be there.

3. LIST VALUES AND PASSIONS

We can look within and ask what we really value and what we are truly passionate about. The intersection of value and passion is often the sweet spot where an individual's purpose lies.

8 ALTRUISM

...or why
we make a life
by what we give

Oregon, in the autumn of 1963. Randle McMurphy, a petty criminal, and social rebel, is transferred for evaluation from a prison farm to a mental institution. But Randle is only faking mental illness because he hopes to evade the prison farm's restrictive environment and hard work.

Randle soon finds that the institution is run by martinet Nurse Ratched, who keeps her patients intimidated through abuse, medication, and sessions of electroconvulsive therapy. Ratched's malicious authority has turned the institution into a restrictive and joyless environment.

McMurphy wants to change things for the good and starts pushing back against the system. Ratched soon sees McMurphy's lively, rebellious presence as a threat to her authority. A battle of wills ensues between the chaotic, freedom-loving McMurphy and the cunning, power-crazed Nurse Ratched.

It culminates in McMurphy instigating an escape, hijacking a bus, and taking all the patients deep-sea fishing on a cruise boat. Most of the patients experience freedom and rebellion for the first time. When they are caught and brought back to the mental institution, McMurphy is treated with electroshock as punishment.

Though he could have easily escaped, McMurphy decides to stay and keep fighting the inhumane conditions. It ends in tragedy for Randle McMurphy; ultimately, he is lobotomized in order to control him and then killed by a fellow inmate in an act of mercy. McMurphy struggled against a system which he had no chance to defeat.

McMurphy did not start out with the intention of being a hero. But when he saw Nurse Ratched humiliating the patients and undermining their recovery from mental diseases, he started fighting for their sanity and eventually sacrificed himself to help others. Yet he did help, for conditions became better. There is a hint at the end that the other patients followed McMurphy's example, and they, too, lived their lives with more self-determination from then on.

This is, of course, the story of the great movie ONE FLEW OVER THE CUCKOO'S NEST, based on the novel by Ken Kesey.

Doing good prolongs lives

There is one trait that all heroes have in common: They always act for the greater good, even when that goes against their self-interest.

They act for the greater good even when they know it could mean failure on a personal level. They are determined to do what is right. They will not stand by and watch the right thing not being done, even if that means sacrificing themselves.

Psychologists call this altruism or pro-social behavior. These terms refer to any action that benefits other people unconditionally, whether the giver benefits from that action or not.

The good news is that helping others and serving the community is not only morally good but also good for our personal wellbeing.

There is a Chinese proverb that goes: "If you want happiness for an hour, take a nap. If you want happiness for a day, go fishing. If you want happiness for a year, inherit a fortune. If you want happiness for a lifetime, help somebody."

Mirroring this Chinese wisdom, there is indeed overwhelming evidence from scientific studies that helping others reduces stress, promotes positive changes in the brain associated with happiness, and benefits our physical health.

Allan Luks did a long-term study on the subject. He termed the physical benefits of volunteering and helping others "the helper's high." His research concluded that regular helpers are ten times more likely to be in good health than people who don't volunteer. (19)

Even better, doing good and helping others can prolong our lives. Researchers from the University of Buffalo found, in a study from 2013, a link between giving selflessly and a lower risk of early death. (20)

Also, helping others often inspires us to lead a more physically active lifestyle, distracts us from our own problems, and improves our self-esteem and competence.

Helping enriches our lives on a social level. Through serving the community, we meet people we normally wouldn't meet. Being part of a social group leads to a feeling of belonging and helps reduce loneliness and isolation.

Finally, helping others allows us to build up a memory bank of doing good for others. That will enable us to look back in harmony and gratitude and motivates us to do good again.

Sounds very alluring, doesn't it? But there is more to it. Selfless service doesn't only benefit the individual; it is also infectious and benefits society as a whole.

Create a ripple

A research study conducted by Stanford psychologists in

2014 found that altruistic behavior is often triggered more by relationships than by instincts. (21)

This is called the "ripple effect." Like ripples expanding across the water when an object is dropped into it, good deeds will reach others and be passed on.

If we set a good example and are frontrunners of good deeds, others will be encouraged to repeat those good deeds. This continuous loop of good deeds eventually leads to a happier and better community.

Science writer Elizabeth Svoboda found in her research about altruism that "what we need and what the world needs are very often one and the same." (22) There is a lot of truth to that because altruism is very often a win-win situation. Through the sheer act of helping, we not only benefit somebody else but benefit ourselves through what we learn in the process. Everybody wins.

Don't give fish. Teach how to fish

We can see that there is much convincing evidence that doing good, and serving the greater good, is worthwhile in every respect– for ourselves, our environment, and society as a whole.

The beauty is, that it is easy. Anyone can start right now to go out and help others. Start small. Volunteer. Help in the local soup kitchen. Share skills and knowledge. Be a mentor. Set a good example.

The gift of time is often more valued and more satisfying than the gift of money. We obviously do not all have the same amount of money, but we all have time on our hands and can all pass along our skills. "Don't give the people fish. Teach them how to fish."

Care about others and draw strength from doing so. A shared purpose gives us strength. Anyone who holds a leadership responsibility can set a good example and define the norm for helping behavior within their group. The effect will ripple outward.

Heroes act for the greater good

Looking deeper into the lives of heroes, it becomes apparent that all heroes have one thing in common: They believe there is something more important than themselves. They would sacrifice themselves for the greater good, for the community, for a good cause, or for people they love.

Think of one of the most famous modern-day heroines: Katniss Everdeen in THE HUNGER GAMES, an adventure tale set in a dystopian future. To protect her younger sister Primrose, Katniss volunteers to take part in a deadly game against physically superior opponents. Katniss takes part in this game even though she knows it could mean her death.

Katniss survives the games' ordeal and creates a ripple effect by giving the oppressed villagers something they lost a long time ago: hope. Not only has Katniss challenged the inhumane government of this world, The Capitol, but she has also demonstrated that they can indeed be beaten at their own game. Such an impossibility creates hope among her people and eventually sets off the long-needed rebellion.

ERIN BROCKOVICH is another example of a hero acting for the greater good. She puts her own personal and professional life in danger to help her community by exposing the evil deeds of a chemical corporation.

In the disaster movie ARMAGEDDON, the character Harry Stamper makes the ultimate sacrifice: his own life. A giant asteroid is approaching Earth and will undoubtedly kill millions. In the end, the only way to stop the asteroid is to manually detonate a nuclear weapon on its surface and split it into two pieces. Harry, an ordinary driller, volunteers to detonate the bomb while on the asteroid and thus prevent it from ever reaching Earth. He sacrifices himself for the greater good.

Sometimes a hero who acts for the greater good is not even human. Think of the lovable robot called THE IRON GIANT in the animated movie of the same name. When the military accidentally fires an atomic bomb at a village, the Iron Giant flies off into space to intercept the bomb with his body. He sacrifices himself for the greater good.

There are real-life people such as Gandhi, and Spartacus, and William Wallace as seen in BRAVEHEART, who sacrificed their own lives for the greater good and whose legacy lives on to the present day. People still walk in their footsteps and do good deeds because these heroes set such a great example.

And it doesn't have to be world-saving big things. Remember George Bailey in IT'S A WONDERFUL LIFE. He does many small good things for his community and thus changes everyone's lives for the better. By his actions, he motivates his fellow villagers to do good themselves.

The list goes on and on. The bottom line is that heroes serve the greater good and put themselves second. Otherwise, they wouldn't be heroes.

Suffering can create altruism

Interestingly, selfless service and altruism are often born out of suffering. Many scientific studies are suggesting that people who go through severe hardship in their lives are more likely to give and help others. The psychologist Philip Zimbardo found that survivors of a disaster or personal trauma are six times more likely to be heroes and volunteers. (23)

Think about it: When we suffer and eventually heal, we go through a psychological transformation and start empathizing with the people who suffer themselves. That is because we have been there and experienced it first-hand.

This gets mirrored by many Heroes' Journeys; the hero often goes through a deep valley of pain before devoting her or his life to the greater good.

Peter Parker, aka SPIDERMAN, was a nerdy kid who was

bullied in school. Bruce Wayne, aka BATMAN, was traumatized as a child by watching his parents get killed by a mugger. Real-life heroes such as Martin Luther King, Jr. and Nelson Mandela had to undergo extreme suffering before they set out on their humane missions.

The lesson here is that instead of drowning in self-pity and trying to numb our pain, we should face our misery head-on, turn our pain into purpose, and use our past experience of suffering to help others.

As the Buddhist nun Pema Chodron writes: "When we feel wretched, that softens us up. It ripens our hearts. It becomes the ground for understanding others."

We're a multi-billionaire? Great. But how do we treat other people?

When we stop thinking primarily about ourselves, we can undergo a truly heroic transformation of consciousness. We won't find true happiness if we don't care about other people and the greater good.

It is not necessary to win in the end to make life good; however, it *is* necessary to invest in an ideal to follow and fight for what is right. There can be beauty in the tragedy of self-sacrifice; just ask the millions of people who call TITANIC their favorite movie or ROMEO AND JULIET the play of their choice.

In the end, we're all in this together. All of us. Every single person on this planet. We are part of a larger whole, and together we can try to move this world's progress a little bit farther forward every day.

The stakes for us are high when it comes to living a truly heroic life. But for our beautiful planet as a whole, the stakes are even higher. Each of us can make a difference if we take the right opportunity to help others. The opportunities out there are almost infinite, so there is no excuse not to go into action. Sometimes all it takes is to look beyond our own existence and find something out there worth fighting for.

Ultimately, selflessness will create something bigger than ourselves and will live on long after we are gone. It is refreshing and energizing to work on a project that is larger than ourselves and could last for generations to come.

Listen to Winston Churchill himself: "We make a living by what we get; we make a life by what we give."

True words. So, give! Heroes do.

FOR THE IMPATIENT AND HURRIED

Three ways to create a ripple:

1. START SMALL

Go out and do simple acts of kindness. They will ripple.

2. GIVE THE GIFT OF TIME

Pass skills on to others. Don't give the people fish; teach them how to fish.

3. SHARE A PURPOSE

A shared purpose gives us strength; we draw strength from caring about others.

9 RESPONSIBILITY

...or why being accountable
is a choice

January 15, 2009. The US Airways pilots Capt. Chesley "Sully" Sullenberger and his first officer, Jeffrey Skiles, board their Airbus A320 at LaGuardia Airport for a routine flight to Charlotte, North Carolina. The two experienced pilots had done this flight many times previously. On a normal day, the flight time was just under two hours.

But on this day, nothing is normal.

Three minutes into the flight, a flock of Canada geese smash into the plane and disable both jet engines. Sully has to react fast. He only has 208 seconds, and there isn't time to peruse any emergency manuals.

He does not follow the "normal" procedure for such an incident, which involves returning to the nearest airport. Instead, Capt. Sullenberger attempts a spectacular emergency landing right on the Hudson River, a maneuver that had never been considered before.

But Sully succeeds in landing the disabled plane on the river and manages to save the lives of all 155 passengers. This feat would later be celebrated as one of the most astounding and improbable emergency landings in the history of civil aviation.

Instead of celebrating Sully as a hero, the National Transportation Safety Board (NTSB) claims at first that several computerized flight simulations showed he could have safely landed the plane at a nearby airport. They believe the accident may have been due to pilot error, which would end Sully's career immediately.

Sully insists that the simulations have to be re-run with live pilots under realistic conditions. Indeed, these simulations end in crashes and the potential loss of all passengers. Even though a river landing might have been an unorthodox solution, Sully took the best option available and saved everybody's life. His career and reputation are fully rehabilitated.

This is the story of Steven Spielberg's SULLY, based on real events.

What did Capt. Sullenberger do? He took 100% responsibility and accountability for his actions during and after the incident, and did what he thought was the right thing to do. He acted against all "normal" advice, and against all the emergency procedures, he was taught in countless flight simulator training sessions.

The lesson here is: heroes hold themselves accountable for their actions and do not shy away from their responsibilities.

Be the creator of circumstances

But what do responsibility and its sibling, accountability, actually mean? They mean the willingness to stand up and be counted. They mean taking the initiative and delivering on a commitment.

Responsibility means acknowledging the choices we have and acting on them while taking charge of all consequences.

Accountability is keeping promises and doing what we say we will do.

Imagine the opposite of responsibility for a moment: That would be passively waiting for our fate to be determined by luck or others. In that case, we would solely depend on external forces to dictate our future. Doesn't sound too appealing, does it?

The advantages of behaving responsibly and accountably are vast and essential for our lives. By doing so, we empower ourselves to make a difference. We take our destiny into our own hands and grow the confidence to make things better. We are the creators, not the victims, of circumstances.

In the *Handbook of the Sociology of Mental Health,* sociology professors Catherine E. Ross and John Mirowsky of the University of Texas found that if we believe our focus of control lies internally– meaning we take accountability for our actions– we experience lower levels of psychological distress, as opposed to people who believe external forces determine our actions. (24)

Also, we become better problem-solvers when we take accountability for the mistakes we make. Through the act of acknowledging our mistakes, we take the first step in learning from those mistakes and have a chance to do better the next time.

When we take responsibility for our mistakes, we are forced to reflect on our own behavior and motivations. It has the nice by-product of making us learn about ourselves the hard way. It helps us identify who we really are, which is an important prerequisite for personal growth.

The hero who has given up being right at all costs is rewarded with liberation. Being able to admit to mistakes and not having to be right all the time lifts a big weight from us and releases good energy that we can use somewhere else.

Holding ourselves accountable can have a positive effect on social affairs, too. Owning our mistakes and actions enhances our relationships, because people find us more trustworthy and can better relate to us.

Why we avoid responsibility

The big question: If acting responsibly and taking accountability only bring advantages, then why do people so often avoid them?

On a superficial level, avoiding responsibility can make our lives *seem* easier. If things go wrong, we can blame our hard upbringing or other disadvantages we might have experienced. We can point our fingers at others and blame them. Parents and educational systems are convenient targets for people who avoid taking accountability for their actions. We can be completely in denial about the mistakes we have made, which can conveniently avoid short-term confrontation.

It is human nature that we don't like to be reminded of our wrongdoings and don't like to admit our flaws to others.

There is also a psychological phenomenon called the "bystander effect." That means we are less likely to take action in a crisis when part of a larger group of people, as we tend to hang back and rely on other members of the group to take the initiative. (25)

But think about the bad consequences. By not owning our mistakes, by not being accountable for our flaws, there is a real danger that we will not learn from them. Then we end up making the very same mistakes over and over again. Even worse, we might adopt a wrong self-conception by lying to ourselves and, thus, have no room to improve and grow.

By removing ourselves from a potential role in the problem, we also remove ourselves from the potential solution. That, in turn, takes from us the satisfaction and joy of solving problems and overcoming hurdles ourselves.

Simply put: If we always blame other people and external circumstances for our shortcomings or misfortunes, we give up our power to learn, grow, and change.

How to learn responsibility

The good news is that we can learn responsibility. That starts with asking ourselves if there is anything we try to avoid or hide in our lives. Going out and confronting those things is the next step in taking full responsibility for it. Always remember that responsibility is a choice.

Another way to learn responsibility is to change our mindset. We can continuously make ourselves aware that we are in total control of our actions and thoughts. Next time feelings of blame or guilt come up in difficult situations, recognize that both might be signs of evading responsibility. We can step back and examine how our own actions have affected that situation.

In fact, we liberate our lives when we stop running and hiding from mistakes. Taking responsibility and owning our mistakes will make our lives truthful and authentic. Things might be harder in the short term but pay off in the long term. We will all be more honest, especially with ourselves.

Heroes and responsibility

Looping back to heroes: They take responsibility and hold themselves accountable for their actions. Otherwise, they wouldn't be heroes.

Take the movie GOOD NIGHT AND GOOD LUCK, based on the true story of courageous broadcast journalist Edward R. Murrow during the gloomy days of the McCarthy era. Mr. Murrow takes responsibility and encourages his viewers to stand up to the persecution of innocent people. In the politically toxic environment of 1950s America, he puts his own life at risk, stays true to his character, and holds himself accountable for his own actions. In the end, his brave and honest broadcasts helped to censure Senator Joseph McCarthy.

WALL-E, one of the most adorable Pixar characters, is another prime example of a hero who takes responsibility. This innocent little robot is programmed to collect waste, which was left behind on the deserted planet Earth. He fulfils his job with utmost responsibility and always does his best no matter what he is doing– even though no one is watching. It is a lonely and mundane job, but

WALL-E manages to find happiness in the smallest of things.

Later in the story, WALL-E takes responsibility for his friend and love interest, the female robot EVE, and helps her no matter what. He then teaches the remaining members of the human race that they can come back to planet Earth and be accountable for the damage they caused. WALL-E is a universal reminder that we, as the human race, are responsible for the wellbeing of the planet that we live on.

The 1973 cop thriller SERPICO, based on true events, is the story of snotty but incorruptible policeman Frank Serpico. He slowly finds out that most of his friends and colleagues in the police department are corrupt. Serpico decides to take responsibility and blows the whistle on the corrupt cops around him. Though his fellow cops and friends threaten him, he stays true to himself and remains 100% accountable for his actions.

Be a creator, not a victim

Life is full of choices. Ultimately the stories of our lives will be the result of the choices we make and the actions we take. People who act responsibly believe they can shape their lives. They attribute events and conditions, whether good or bad, to their very own choices and deeds.

We can choose to be the creators of our destiny. We can seek solutions, take action, and try something new when prompted with a stimulus from our environment. Or we can choose to be the victim of our world, blaming, complaining, and finding excuses for everything that goes wrong.

The former helps us to achieve our goals and leads to autonomy. The latter seldom helps us to accomplish either one.

Of course, there is no guarantee that we will achieve all of our objectives. But once we take responsibility for our actions, we have a greater chance of creating the life we desire.

Listen to Bob Dylan's words: "A hero is someone who understands the responsibility that comes with his freedom."

We must be responsible for everything we do. We should not be victims but responsible creators. Heroes are.

FOR THE IMPATIENT AND HURRIED

Three ways to learn more responsibility:

1. DETECT AVOIDANCE AND HIDING

We can ask ourselves if there is anything we try to avoid or hide in our lives. Once we identified it, we should own and take responsibility for it.

2. CHANGE OUR MINDSET

We should make ourselves aware that we are in total control of our actions; and if feelings of guilt and shame creep up, we should ask ourselves if those are signs of evaded responsibility.

3. OWN OUR MISTAKES

If we make a mistake, we need to own it. Only then can we learn from it and improve.

PART III

ID

the instinctual desirer

10 COURAGE

...or why
fear holds
the treasure
we seek

Clarice Starling is a young FBI cadet in training. She is extremely intelligent and ambitious, regularly achieving the highest results in her class. But she has also a troubled mind; her father died early, and she lived through traumatic childhood experiences that still haunt her. By achieving greatness in her job and hunting down criminals, she hopes to silence the dark voices in her head.

One day Clarice is pulled from her training in Virginia for an assignment at a high-security facility at Baltimore State Hospital. There she has to interview the cannibalistic serial killer Hannibal Lecter, in an effort to get some useful insights that might help the FBI to catch a psychopathic slaughterer nicknamed Buffalo Bill.

Clarice is intimidated by the evil mastermind Hannibal, but likewise fascinated by his intellectual brilliance and wit. Hannibal is only willing to help her with insights about the case if Clarice, in exchange, tells him about her past and personal trouble. Tit for tat. Psychological mind games ensue, which force Clarice to face her own demons.

With the Hannibal's help, Clarice is eventually lead to Buffalo Bill's creepy house, which is packed with mannequins, stuffed moths, and rows of chemical jars. She slowly descends into the basement with a gun outstretched before her.

Suddenly the light goes out. It is pitch black. All of the sounds are magnified. Moths fly into her face. She keeps creeping through the dark, knowing that the killer is somewhere in the house. She is trembling. Her hands are sweating. Her pupils are dilated. Her heart beats out of her chest, and she gasps for air.

Like all heroes in extreme situations, Clarice feels fear.

This is the story of the superb thriller THE SILENCE OF THE LAMBS.

The interesting thing about fear

Though Clarice Starling is as courageous and ambitious as it gets, she still feels fear.

Fear is the most infamous of basic human emotions. We all feel fear. Fear will never leave us; it is our lifelong companion, so, we had better get used to it.

In fact, anxiety disorders are the most common mental health diagnoses and affect one in five people in the western world.

In the USA, home of the loud and the bold, the most common fear is, ironically, glossophobia – fear of public speaking. A staggering 74% of Americans suffer from glossophobia, followed by 68% of Americans who suffer from necrophobia – fear of death. (26)

This is quite staggering when we know that we are born with only two innate fears, both of which keep us alive as toddlers: the fear of falling and the fear of loud sounds. With all other fears, we learn and adopt them on our journey called life.

A learned and adopted fear not only affects our mind but our body. It typically causes an accelerated heart rate, shallow breath, dizziness, sweating, increase in adrenaline, and other symptoms. We often interpret these sensations as signaling danger.

But what is fear, really? One of the most basic definitions of fear says it is "an emotion triggered by a perceived threat." But wait– let's retake a look at the definition. It says that fear is triggered by a ***perceived*** threat, not an actual one. The word ***perceived*** implies that we only fear a ***possible*** outcome even though there might not be any real danger.

Here's the paradox: Approximately 99% of the fear people experience today is non-physical. It is fear that only exists in our heads. However, even though it cannot hurt us or kill us, it can do a lot of harm to us. It messes with our confidence. It can take a toll on our mental health. It makes us avoid acting the way we want to act because we fear the potential bad consequences.

Thus, fear can keep us from living the life we want to live. It can prevent us from doing the things we love and from loving the things we do.

Avoidance amplifies fear

Understandably, but unfortunately, most people try to avoid situations or people that they fear.

From a psychological standpoint, avoidance is the worst thing we can do when dealing with fear because it prevents our nervous system from "habituating." That means if we do not confront the feared object or situation, it remains novel to our brain and keeps on provoking the same anxiety.

Even worse, avoiding what we are afraid of tends to generalize it over time. For example, if we avoid attending one meeting because of anxiety, we might end up avoiding all meetings. The dilemma with avoidance is that it often creates the very outcome we are trying to avoid. Doesn't sound too appealing, does it?

And it gets worse. Every time we avoid something, we fear, we tend to experience a sense of failure. Our anxiety gains strength while we overall lose strength.

Avoidance also eliminates practice. Without practice, it is difficult to gain mastery. Without mastery, confidence is less likely to rise.

We are hopefully convinced by now that avoiding what we fear is not good at all. Avoidance not only maintains our fear; it amplifies it.

Fear will be always there - and that is a good thing

And there is no real point of trying to avoid fear because fear will always be with us anyway; and this is not a bad thing.

The truth is that we need fear. Fear is an essential and useful part of our lives. It alerts us to danger, identifies threats, and brings out our survival instinct. It is a response that allowed the human species to survive thousands of years, despite wars, natural disasters, and all kinds of predators. Fear was designed to keep us safe and alive. In other words, fear is human and completely normal.

When something terrifies us, our eyes widen and allow us to see the threat more clearly. At the same time, our hearts begin to beat faster, pumping much-needed blood to the rest of our bodies. Adrenaline prepares us to either fight or escape the threat.

Also, fear can be quite an arousing sensation. Remember all the exciting video nights in our teenage years when we snuggled up on our parents' sofas with friends and deliberately exposed ourselves to fear with the latest horror flicks? The sensation of fear is actually drug-like; intense fear causes the brain to release chemicals that mimic the effects of marijuana and amphetamines.

To sum up, fear cannot be eradicated, nor should it. But it does have to be managed, because fear can be damaging to our lives when it prevents us from doing what we need to do or want to do.

Face fear – and it will diminish

So, if fear is always there but it is bad to avoid it, what do we do with our fears? The best way to manage fear is to face it. If we face it, it will diminish.

Every time we confront our fear, we gain power while our anxiety loses. Every time we confront our fear, we gain evidence of our ability to cope. Every time we confront our fear, we gain a sense of accomplishment and empowerment. If we do this repeatedly, we will get a sense of mastery that reduces the angst of failure.

Exposure isn't easy. But living in a life-long prison of avoidance is worse. And sometimes, it takes only a few seconds to overcome our fear.

The character Benjamin in the comedy film WE BOUGHT A ZOO is a nervous wreck when he first sees his love interest, Kelly. But it takes just twenty seconds of courage to go talk to her. If he had avoided these twenty seconds spent overcoming his fear, he would have never met the love of his life.

"We know," Benjamin says, "that sometimes all we need is twenty seconds of insane courage. Just literally twenty seconds of embarrassing bravery. I promise, something great will come of it."

To reiterate: Fear mostly exists in our minds only– the fear of failing, the fear of getting old, the fear of dying. We either face those fears or cringe in front of them and if we cringe, we end up becoming only a fragment of who we could be.

Courage is not the absence of fear

To overcome fear, one virtue is of extreme importance: courage.

It is important to understand that being courageous doesn't mean being fearless. Courage is not the absence of fear but moving ahead in spite of it. Courage is an existential choice we take. It is an empowering experience to stand up when we are afraid, and the odds are against us.

The word "courage" comes from the French *coeur*, which means heart. Courageous actions should come from the heart.

Remember the Scottish freedom fighter William Wallace in BRAVEHEART? It took all his courage and all his heart to overcome his fears and fight the ruthless English.

In LORD OF THE RINGS, the hobbit Frodo was fearful all the way to Mordor. Even the mighty wizard Gandalf felt fear when he heard the orcs' distant drums down in the dark mines of Moria. But our heroes were courageous enough to continue their journey to Mount Doom in order to fulfil their destiny.

Standing up to evil and fighting for what we truly believe in takes courage, especially when it places one's own physical safety or that of one's family at risk.

A certain amount of courage is required in almost every human activity or endeavor. Getting old demands courage. To allow oneself to love and commit to another person takes courage. To artistically express ourselves takes courage. Making changes to our careers or relationships requires courage. There is no meaningful life without courage. At all.

There is beauty and nobility in courageously facing what we fear, and that can be contagious. Think of great leaders like Alexander the Great or Spartacus, who always led the way on the battlefield by fighting in the first row and thus inspiring armies of men to follow them.

Listen to the Greek philosopher Aristotle, who believed courage to be the most important quality we have. "Courage is the first of human virtues, because it makes all others possible."

Heroes and fear

Heroes feel fear, as we all do. They feel the same intense emotional sensations that we do when they fear. Do heroes ever get rid of their fear? Most likely not. Some heroes even suffer from very irrational fears.

X-Men's WOLVERINE might be the ultimate comic book badass. He is basically invincible but also suffers from a very common fear: aerophobia, the fear of flying.

Indiana Jones fights Nazi ghost-demons, is chased by giant boulders and is confronted by aggressive bird spiders. But there is one thing he is genuinely terrified by: snakes. Indy suffers from ophidiophobia.

Our beloved PETER PAN suffers from gerascophobia, which is the fear of growing old.

DON QUIXOTE, one of the classic heroes in literature, suffers from pragmatophobia, the fear of reality.

The sheriff in JAWS suffers from thalassophobia, the fear of open water, which becomes very impractical when hunting down a great white shark in the Atlantic Ocean.

The list goes on. All heroes have fears and anxieties of some sort. But does fear stop heroes from doing the right thing? Does fear paralyze them and put them into a life-long standstill? The answer, of course, is no. Heroes go into action and face their fears.

"The hero and the coward both feel the same thing: fear. It's what they do with that fear that separates them."

Heroes not only face the fears which are down in the deepest part of their soul, they also grow and learn through them. They come back with a gift and grow through their experience. The famous mythologist Joseph Campbell rightly said, "The cave we fear to enter holds the treasure we seek." (27)

Take Marlin in FINDING NEMO. He is terribly scared of the open sea since his spouse was killed by a predator's attack. Now he is overprotective of his young son, Nemo, and anxious about everything Nemo does.

But at a crucial moment, Marlin is ready to face his biggest fears. He swims through the whole ocean and dodges sharks. When Nemo is trapped in an enormous fishing net, Marlin does the bravest thing any parent can do: He trusts his child to save himself. In the end, Marlin not only has his son back, but he's rewarded with a less anxious and more fulfilling life.

Take Ron from HARRY POTTER. He is so deeply scared of spiders that he freezes in fearful pain when he sees them. However, when poor Hermione is turned to stone, Ron overcomes his fears and boldly faces those terrifying eight-legged creatures.

Remember Scottie Ferguson in Alfred Hitchcock's masterpiece VERTIGO? Scottie is a former detective who suffers from acrophobia, the fear of heights. Only by facing this fear and dragging his love interest all the way up to the top of a tall church tower, is he eventually able to solve the mystery and reveal the sad truth.

Heroes pass on their courage to others. Courage can be infectious.

Remember the adorable Pixar character from UP: Ellie Fredricksen. From early childhood she is a gutsy little girl, courageously exploring her surroundings and never avoiding any adventures or fearful situations. Her dream is to go on an adventurous trip to Paradise Falls at the other end of the world.

However, every time she and her husband, Carl, have saved enough money for the trip, the more mundane things of life get in the way: a car repair, a leaking roof, a hospital bill. When they finally buy the tickets and are ready to fulfil their dreams, Ellie, unfortunately, falls ill.

On her deathbed, Ellie hands all her bravery to her life partner, the timid and somewhat fearful Carl. She asks him not to spend the rest of his life mourning her but to spend it on adventures instead. And so, Carl does; he leaves with his home to go to a foreign country and has many adventures, the direct result of Ellie's contagious bravery.

The greatest treasures are guarded by our greatest fears

Most of our ambitious goals are on the other side of fear.

Anxiety must be lived through if we want to achieve our goals. Most avoidance and coping tactics only end in misery.

The beauty is that after each event of fear, there will also be a reward. What was previously avoided has now been done. If we confront what we fear, we will get growing evidence that we can be more than we thought we could be– regardless of the outcome.

Heroes who have faced and pushed through their fears often see the world, and themselves, differently after that. They realize that they can be a different person from what they always thought they would be. What was once thought impossible has now been proven to be possible. Even attempting the seemingly impossible can have a transformative effect on us.

In short: what we fear doing most is very often what we most need to do.

Conclusion

As we learned in the chapter about proactivity, we most regret the things we *haven't* done. Avoiding our fears and refusing to pursue our dream is terminal. We will end up with a life without joy, commitment, or fulfilment.

Fear is in all of us. It is an ever-present emotion. Heroes accept this fact and follow their path anyway. Overcoming fear makes us stronger. Always be courageous. Fear of failure leads to wasted talent.

Benjamin Franklin once said, "Most people die at twenty-five and are buried at seventy-five." For some people, this metaphorical death — when they decide to settle for a mediocre lifestyle — comes even earlier than that. These people are so afraid of living the life they want that they end up quitting in advance, because they fear risking failure. Not trying at all seems, to them, to be the safer option.

We have seen in the chapter about rule-breaking that people are hard-wired for personal connections. Indeed, vast psychological research suggests that at the heart of avoidance is often the fear of rejection. (28) Rejection in all its forms (being dropped, fired, left out, suspended, divorced, isolated, made redundant, ostracized, laughed at, etc.) can trigger a strong death-like reaction.

We hate it, and we intuitively do anything we can to avoid this pain. Ironically, the attempts to play it safe only result in more fear and more isolation.

The hero, on the other hand, risks rejection all the time. A hero realizes that turning away from fear – pretending, being silent, or remaining obedient– carries a high price, for it obstructs the road to independence, choice, and freedom. A hero knows that rejection, though scary, is not the end of the world but can be the beginning of something new.

We often avoid relatively easy situations– talking to somebody we like, asking our boss for a pay raise, or showing up to that meeting– only because we fear we might look foolish. But isn't looking foolish an incredibly small price to pay to do what we want and live a more fulfilled life?

Did Maverick in TOP GUN fear to look foolish when he started singing a song for his love interest, Charlie, in the middle of a lively restaurant? Maybe he did; but singing he did anyway and won the heart of the love of his life.

Be audacious in the pursuit of our dreams. Be courageous and look foolish. Remember, there is no such thing as fearlessness. Even the greatest heroes feel fear. It's just that at some point on their journey, they decide to face and overcome their fears.

Fear might be the most powerful obstacle any of us will ever face in our lives. But overcoming it will reward us with the greatest gifts in life. Facing our fear and being courageous ultimately determines what we do with our lives– and what we don't do.

We must throw all avoidance and coping strategies overboard and face our fears. Heroes do.

FOR THE IMPATIENT AND HURRIED

Three steps to becoming more courageous:

1. WE SHOULD MAKE IT A HABIT TO SAY WHAT WE THINK

When we have a different opinion about something, that opinion must be said. Say it pleasantly and politely, but say it with conviction and don't swallow it.

2. FACE OUR FEARS REGULARLY

We must ask ourselves what we are afraid of and then face those things on a regular basis. Count down from three and get into action. Courage is a muscle we can build. Fear diminishes the more often we face it.

3. THINK OF OURSELVES LESS

We feel fear the most when we are self-conscious and think about our own thoughts and feelings too much. Instead, we can focus outwards and act on a cause or group of people we care about. Courage is strongest when we are courageous for something or someone else.

11 SHADOWS
...or why we should
visit the wild things

A young boy named Bruce Wayne is enjoying an untroubled and happy upbringing as an only child. His very wealthy parents, Thomas and Martha, are loving and caring towards their son and devoted to providing him with the best possible education.

One day, young Bruce's blissful childhood takes a sharp and unexpected turn to the dark side. He falls into a dry well where he is attacked by a swarm of bats, which traumatizes him and triggers a lifelong fear of bats. Days later he attends an opera performance with his parents, where he is so frightened by the performers' bat costumes that he begs his parents to leave. Then, on a side street outside of the opera house, Bruce witnesses the murder of his parents by a mugger.

Orphaned at the age of eight, Bruce is brought up by the family butler, Alfred. Throughout his childhood and teenage years, he remains a traumatized outsider driven by guilt, fear, and anger. As a young adult, he tracks down his parents' murderer and decides to kill him, but an assassin from a rival mafia clan kills the man first.

In a moment of insight, Bruce leaves his old life behind and embarks on a seven-year-long trip around the world to channel and control his dark character traits. After being steeled through immersion in the underworld and through high-intensity combat training, Bruce finally returns home. Intending to eradicate the evil in his crime-ridden hometown of Gotham City, Bruce re-invents himself as the vigilante superhero Batman.

This is the story of BATMAN BEGINS.

During the day, he is Bruce Wayne, a wealthy American playboy, philanthropist, and owner of Wayne Enterprises. At night he becomes The Batman, a dark knight, and vigilante who hunts down criminals.

Bruce Wayne says at one point in the story, "I guess we're all two people: the one in daylight and the one we keep in shadow." He is referring to what are called, in psychological terms, the shadow traits. Batman, and heroes in general, do face their shadows.

But what is the "shadow" really? It is the unknown "dark side" of our personality. It consists mainly of primitive, negative human emotions and impulses such as sexual lust, rage, envy, greed, selfishness, desire, and anger. As this part of us is not visible from the outset, Swiss psychiatrist Carl Jung coined it our "shadow."

Jungian analyst Aniela Jaffe defined the shadow more precisely as the "sum of all personal and collective psychic elements which, because of their incompatibility with the chosen conscious attitude, are denied expression in life." (29)

Whereas some of our character traits are very obvious and open, others are rather hidden. And it is often these hidden shadow traits that we don't want to deal with, because those are the traits which can be dark, off the norm, and evil.

Psychological research suggests that if we want to understand the sheer endless complexity of our lives, we must first understand our inner self and everything that comes with it. (30) In this case, "everything" means we have to deal with aspects of ourselves that are not easy to face.

Suppressing magnifies

Think about it: From early childhood, society and our immediate environment teach us to keep certain emotions and character traits under wraps. That's because some traits are regarded as being not very civilized and are not accepted by our society.

As children, when we expressed certain parts of ourselves, we often received negative and restrictive feedback from people around us. Thus, we tame ourselves and hide our dark impulses. We learn to be civilized and norm-abiding members of what we think is a "normal" society.

We suppress our unwanted dark parts to the point that they become entirely eradicated from our conscious mind.

However, suppressing and ignoring our shadow doesn't mean it is not there anymore. That suppression pushes it from our conscious awareness and keeps it hidden in a dark corner of the mind. It is much like a window on a computer that we minimize, but it still keeps operating unseen in the background.

As the poet Robert Bly rightly says, "The child puts all of these unwanted parts into an invisible bag and drags it behind him into adulthood." (31)

The bad news is that anything that is resisted or suppressed will only get bigger and look for release. Any part of us we disown can turn against us. Our shadow is merely a collection of these unwanted parts inside us. It is our enemy within.

Projections and their inherent danger

The bigger issue: Our shadow can affect us against our will and without our full consciousness. It is as if we are temporarily on autopilot. When the shadow is in control, we may have outbursts of negative emotions and behaviors. We may do and say things we do not like and later regret our words and actions.

The other big danger of suppressing and ignoring our dark

side is called, in psychology, "projection." This is an unconscious defense mechanism where we project negative parts of ourselves onto others and thereby scapegoat them. For example: If we are annoyed by someone else's rudeness or anger, there is a high likelihood that this is a dark trait we ourselves suppress.

But these projections distort reality. They can create a dangerous mismatch between how we perceive ourselves and how we behave in reality.

Remember John Steinbeck's masterpiece EAST OF EDEN? The story centers around the lone farmer Adam Trask, who always prefers his son Aron over his son Cal. Trask makes Cal the scapegoat and black sheep of the family. In other words, Trask projects his shadow – his unconscious anger and disappointment about himself– onto poor Cal.

There is a similar constellation in Arthur Miller's equally significant piece of literature, DEATH OF A SALESMAN. Its protagonist, the unfortunate travelling salesman Willy Loman, projects his bad hidden traits onto his son, Biff. This eventually determines his tragic fate. Projection, unfortunately, happens all too often in father-son relationships.

Sometimes there is collective projection. This happens in TO KILL A MOCKINGBIRD, where the innocent Tom Robinson is made a victim of racial collective scapegoating. It takes a quintessential hero like Atticus Finch to reinstate justice.

Japanese author Haruki Murakami said, "Just as all people have shadows, every society and nation, too, has shadows. If there are bright, shining aspects, there will definitely be a counterbalancing dark side."

And Mr. Murakami is right. The dark chapter of Nazi Germany taught us what can happen when a whole society starts projecting and scapegoating a minority: It gets very inhumane and dangerous.

Drag your shadow into the light

What is the way out of this dilemma?

The answer is: Rather than suppressing our shadow we should drag it into the light instead. We should make it visible. We must know it and own it. We have to appreciate that the shadow is part of ourselves and makes us complete as a person. As Jung writes, "There is no light without shadow and no psychic wholeness without imperfection."

The light cannot exist without the dark. Only by facing our dark sides and balancing them with our positives will harmony be created within us.

The message here is clear: We must visit our shadow, embrace it, learn from it, and master it. That is how we become a complete person driven towards self-acknowledgement and integrity, and away from projection and the scapegoating of others.

Only then will we be able to ***deal with*** our dark emotions instead of ***becoming*** our dark emotions. We will embrace our flaws and realize that we are by no means perfect– and we will, therefore, no longer fear certain aspects of ourselves. With better self-awareness, we will get a clearer and more accurate perception of the world and our environment.

Finding our whole self is a challenging journey, of course. Who is really keen to visit and acknowledge their negative side? It is a bit like DANTE'S INFERNO: Before making our way out of "hell," we must wander through the dark depths of our inner shadow. This is the complete opposite of many spiritual methods that teach us to deny our pain or to discipline ourselves ascetically.

How do we find our own shadow? A simple trick is to think about what irritates us the most about others, for it is likely that those annoying traits reflect our very own shadow. Identify what kind of fear or hate is behind them, take on their energy, and use it for our journey. People who are the biggest nuisances in our lives may offer us the biggest lessons of all.

Another way to discover our shadow is to spot the actions we take accidentally. Look for Freudian slips, bad habits, and repeated behaviors that become negative patterns in our lives. Especially pay attention to your impulsive behaviors which are done in the heat of the moment. This is normally when the ID takes over and displays your shadow.

No matter what our shadow might be, we must be aware of it, shed light on it, and deal with it.

Heroes and their shadows

What about heroes? Do they deal with their shadows?

Absolutely. They often go down the darkest and deepest parts of their soul, and only then do they become a whole and fully integrated person.

Sometimes a hero must literally face a personified version of their shadow. In FIGHT CLUB, the timid and nameless protagonist meets the raw and ferocious Tyler Durden. Durden carries all the dark traits that our main character suppressed until his own life became entirely mediocre and boring. Only by dealing with his personified shadow could the nameless character become a complete version of himself and find some excitement in his formerly dull life.

The interesting thing about many good stories is that the villain often carries the hero's shadow traits. During the journey, the hero learns that they will become like their nemesis if they cannot master their own dark side.

This is exactly what happens in the movie WALL STREET. A young, ambitious banker called Bud badly wants a highly paid financial career on Wall Street. He meets the glamorous, successful, and highly unscrupulous banker Gordon Gekko, who becomes his dark mentor.

Over the course of the story, Bud realizes that Gordon Gekko is his own shadow self and sees that he will become just as immoral and destructive as Gekko if he doesn't change his course in life. Though Bud is, at first, lured and blinded by Gekko's money and power, he ultimately uses these shadow traits of ruthlessness and cruelty for good. He thus defeats the evil Gekko with his own weapons.

Sometimes it is a secondary character who learns shadow lessons from the main character. In FORREST GUMP, Lieutenant Dan discovers in Forrest his hidden shadow traits like naive optimism and innocence. Those are traits that Lieutenant Dan always suppressed and hated in himself, given his self-conception as a tough soldier. Only when Lieutenant Dan faces and embraces them does he find true happiness.

In some movies, a personified shadow carries character traits that the protagonist envies. In SILENCE OF THE LAMBS, FBI agent Clarice Starling craves the charm, elegance, and polished speech of the serial killer Hannibal Lecter, because those are traits, she never acquired due to her simple upbringing.

Most often, the hero is confronted with his inner shadow and goes through a learning circle. In GROUNDHOG DAY, Phil the weatherman, has to go through an infinite time conundrum and is repeatedly confronted with his own shadow, his selfishness, and cynical arrogance until he finally acknowledges his dark side and manages to balance it with his good characteristics. Only then is he released from this peculiar time capsule.

One of the best and most prominent examples of shadow work can be found in STAR WARS. Both Luke and his father, Anakin, carry an enormously forceful shadow within them. Luke visits his shadow and accepts it as part of himself; from this he learns to master it and turn it into something useful. Anakin, on the other hand, remains unaware of his shadow and fails to control it. He soon turns entirely to the dark side and becomes Darth Vader, almost literally the shadow of his former self.

Play with the wild things

The fabulous children's book WHERE THE WILD THINGS ARE contains a big lesson for all of us. The main character is an angry little boy who gets sent to bed without dinner because he has been naughty again. Instead of suppressing and projecting his anger, he embodies his dark side and goes with the wild monsters– his shadow traits– on a memorable trip. He literally goes "where the wild things are" and comes back a bigger boy.

It is very interesting that our shadows hold not only destructive forces, but likewise powerful elements that can enrich our lives. Think about it: A little grain of aggression can strengthen our assertiveness. A pinch of anger can help our energy level. We just need to control it. Once our shadow is fully integrated into the conscious mind, we become a more robust and better-adjusted person.

For example, one of my shadow traits is that I am extremely impatient. I hate waiting, I overreact when things are not going fast enough, and I sometimes rush into action without giving the situation enough thought.

Since I identified this shadow and dragged it into the light, I can better control it. I remind myself not to push too hard when things are too slow but, instead, try to rationalize the situation. When I have to wait or queue somewhere, I started to enjoy my surroundings more consciously. I also started to meditate, which helps.

But I also discovered that there is some virtue in impatience. It can give me energy and push me to make decisions more quickly than others. Thus, I tried to use my shadow trait to my advantage.

There are endless creative possibilities when we unleash our inner shadow. Some of the most significant cultural movements are based on it. Think of the punk movement, Southern gothic, the Film Noir series, Hieronymus Bosch, or the black paintings by Spanish master Francisco Goya. Many classic masterpieces were made by artists who were, consciously or unconsciously, addressing the shadow side in themselves.

Due to societal or peer pressure, some positive traits like anti-authoritarian behavior, critical thinking, and disobedience might have become buried deep down in our unconsciousness. We have to dig for them, find those hidden traits and embrace them.

We are less than we could be without our shadow. A big part of our energy is trapped because it is labelled by our conscious self as bad and negative. Dig for those buried little treasures and free the wild woman or wild man inside.

Carl Jung again: "Taken in its deepest sense, the shadow is the invisible saurian tail that man still drags behind him. Carefully amputated, it becomes the healing serpent of the mysteries."

GAME OF THRONES character Tyrion Lannister put it more simply: "Once you've accepted your flaws, no one can use them against you."

True words. Now it's time for us to go out and work on our shadows. Heroes do.

FOR THE IMPATIENT AND HURRIED

Three steps to finding our shadow:

1. ANNOYING PEOPLE

Make a list of people who annoy and irritate us most. List their most annoying traits. Some of those traits will turn out to be shadow traits that we are projecting onto them.

2. FREUDIAN SLIPS

Pay special attention to Freudian slips, which are things we do or say subconsciously in the heat of the moment. Chances are, these will reveal some of our shadow traits.

3. JOURNAL DREAMS

According to Jung, our shadow can be found in our dreams and in the archetypes, which appear in those dreams. Keep pen and paper next to our bed, write down your dreams, and analyze them.

12 CURIOSITY

...or why
we should
fish in the dark

"In a hole in the ground, there lived a hobbit." Our hobbit, Bilbo Baggins, enjoyed a quiet life in a green, lush area called the Shire, somewhere on the peaceful fringes of Middle-earth. All the other hobbits lived equally contented and unexciting lives, and so every day seemed to be only a slightly different variation of the day before.

However, Bilbo wanted more. He had itchy feet. He suffered from chronic Wanderlust. He felt a strong desire to leave his village and find out what else was out there. He wanted to know. He was curious about what was happening in the rest of the world.

One day a wizard and some quarrelsome dwarves paid him an unexpected visit and took him on an adventurous journey far away from home. Their journey took them on a path through treacherous lands swarming with orcs, goblins, and man-eating trolls. It took them into the dark forest of Mirkwood where they encountered elves, met the peculiar Gollum, and almost got eaten by giant spiders.

Their journey concluded at the Lonely Mountain, where they had to steal the treasure from the dragon Smaug, which ultimately triggered the climactic battle of the Five Armies.

And this whole epic adventure started with nothing more than a curious hobbit suffering from Wanderlust.

Of course, this is the story of Bilbo Baggins in J.R.R. Tolkien's THE HOBBIT.

Without the hero's curiosity, there be no story

Heroes try new things. They embark on spontaneous adventures, explore new places and people, and generally wander through the world with their eyes wide open. In short, heroes are curious.

Being curious means, we are actively interested in a wide variety of things and genuinely want to know more about the world around us. Curiosity, at its core, is about recognizing and seizing the pleasures that new experiences offer us. It is about finding novelty and meaning even in ordinary matters that look familiar from the outside.

Curiosity finds meaning

There are many advantages to curiosity. Vast academic research and science-backed studies have proven that curiosity can drastically improve the quality of our lives. (32)

Curiosity makes our brain and mind more active. When we are in a state of curiosity, we proactively ask questions and try to find answers. Our mind becomes more observant and inquisitive. Being open to new experiences keeps our brains and minds active and alert, and we anticipate new ideas related to the subject we are curious about. Since our brain is a "muscle", it becomes stronger the more often we activate and train it with curiosity.

Studies have shown that curiosity keeps us young. Staying curious helps to preserve our mental activity later in life. (33) The urge to find novelty keeps the world around us exciting and ever-changing.

Other studies show that we tend to learn faster if we are genuinely curious about the subject matter. Curiosity pushes us to complete knowledge gaps about topics and thus is a basis for intellectual achievement. (34)

Curiosity also fosters creativity, as it creates an openness to the unfamiliar and allows us to find things that are usually not visible at first sight. Curious people tend to generate many more original ideas that are counterintuitive or obscure than people who lack curiosity. In his seminal book, ***Creativity: Flow and the Psychology of Discovery and Invention,*** author Mihaly Csikszentmihalyi identified curiosity as the pivotal trait of a creative thinker. (35)

And it gets even better: A psychological study from 2007 conducted by researchers from the George Mason University and the University of Louisville showed that curiosity helps in finding better purpose and meaning in life. Why? Because the curious mind is always looking for new ideas and concepts to explore. (36)

If we are curious, we often pause on our journey called life and look around to see what else is out there. We are more receptive and more likely to find something that triggers our passion since curiosity is most often the starting point for lifelong interests and hobbies.

Curiosity can be helpful on a social level. Curious people are often better listeners and more empathetic because they are genuinely interested and, of course, curious about other people. That can be beneficial for relationships as we remain involved in our partner's life and its continuous changes. And let's be honest: Who would want to be with somebody who is not interested in our lives?

Similarly, being curious is advantageous for leadership. Having a leader with a hungry mind will enable teams to navigate complexity by continually looking for new things. They will find novelty exciting and quickly become bored with routine.

Uncurious leaders will most likely hold on to old methods they know and thus foster stagnation.

Beware of Pandora's Box

We have seen the advantages of being curious. Are there any disadvantages?

Generally, no, but curious people are more prone to embarking on ill-fated adventures. The need to satisfy our curiosity can be so strong that we disregard potential harmful consequences.

Think of Dr. Frankenstein and his creature. Think about the tale of Icarus. On a more mundane level, think of somebody who wakes up every morning and is super curious about all the new videos of puppies and kittens on YouTube.

"The Pandora Effect" describes doing unfortunate things that are driven by boundless curiosity. The name is derived from the old Greek myth of Pandora, who, driven by curiosity, opened a box left in her care, which then released sickness, death, and other unspecified evils into the world forever.

Researchers from the University of Iowa found out that humans possess an inherent desire to resolve uncertainty even if they expect negative consequences. (37) One sad example of this phenomenon is "rubbernecking," which describes slowing down to turn our heads and gawk at a car crash as we drive past the accident site.

A bit of cost-benefit analysis at times can help keep us using our curiosity for things that are worth pursuing with our precious time. But overall, having a curious mind is a blessing and can enrich our lives on many levels.

Be amazed by everyday things

One question remains: can we learn curiosity? The good news is: Yes, we can.

Curiosity starts by being humble. We enter each situation with a clear mind and do not assume we already know how everything works. Asking questions helps– the words ***what, why, when, who, where, and how*** are the best friends of curious people.

Do not take things at face value. Dig deeper. Ultimately that will help us to overcome prejudices and see things as they really are, not how we expect them to be.

As Neil DeGrasse Tyson wisely put it: "The people who don't ask questions remain clueless throughout their lives."

Write the words ***Don't Assume*** in big friendly letters on the wall. Assumptions are the single biggest killer of curiosity, because they stop us from exploring further.

We can never be afraid to ask questions or admit we don't know something. That can take the greatest courage of all.

Never, ever label something as dull. Instead, we must allow ourselves to dive in and be surprised and amazed by everyday things. If we dig a little deeper, we will find exciting details in almost anything. If we label something as not interesting from the start, we have already closed the door to potentially finding something novel and exciting.

Even if we have to do something as mundane as wait in a queue in a supermarket, we can sharpen our observation skills and give more attention to our environment. Look for small details others might miss: the stain on the ground that resembles an octopus, the lady at the bus stop with this strangely pink overcoat, or the conversations that people behind us are having. The goal is to find the unfamiliar in the familiar. Hidden gems are everywhere.

Artist and composer John Cage should know. "If something is boring after two minutes, try it for four. If it is still boring, then eight. Then sixteen. Then thirty-two. Eventually, one discovers that it is not boring at all."

Another useful method for fostering curiosity is to vary our sources of information and use resources, which represent viewpoints other than our own. Listen to people from a wide variety of backgrounds and beliefs. Mingle with those we usually wouldn't hang out with. Mentoring and volunteering are always useful in that respect, as we meet people we wouldn't meet in our "ordinary" life.

And in case we lost it on our long journey into adulthood, I highly recommend reconnecting with play. Adding some moments of play to our daily tasks naturally builds interest and curiosity. Juggle, draw, do crosswords... anything that is done purely for fun.

Curiosity leads to Wonderland

Heroes are generally curious. Think of all the heroes we've seen in adventure movies.

It was curiosity that made a young girl tumble down the rabbit hole and straight into the fantasy known as ALICE IN WONDERLAND. It was curiosity that made the Darling children follow PETER PAN to Neverland. It was curiosity that made Jim Hawkins sail to TREASURE ISLAND. All of those characters were driven by a curious and open mind.

Think of the hobbits Frodo, Sam, Merry, and Pippin in THE LORD OF THE RINGS. It was partly their curiosity that led them on their journey across the misty mountains, into the mines of Moria, and all the way to Mordor.

As the hobbit Frodo says in THE LORD OF THE RINGS: "Still round the corner, there may wait a new road or a secret gate. And though I often have passed them by, a day will come at last when I shall take the hidden paths that run west of the moon, east of the sun."

The life of curious heroes is far from boring. It's never dull or routine. There are always new things to attract their attention, new paths they can travel, and new people they can meet.

The entire movie AMELIE is driven by its main character's curiosity. It is Amelie's unusual approach, which brings some good chaos to the world around her and eventually makes her neighbors happier.

Speaking of neighbors, in the classic Hitchcock thriller REAR WINDOW the main character is a photographer who is bound to his apartment with a broken leg. He is bored to death by not being able to move. His only view is to his apartment building's courtyard, where he can see his neighbors' windows. Only when he starts being curious about their lives does this fascinating crime story unfold.

Curiosity also can be introspective. We can be curious about finding ourselves, which triggers adventure in the first place. Think of all the movies about self-discovery.

In the film WILD, a woman named Cheryl has a sad history of mental and physical abuse. To fight her past demons, Cheryl embarks on a thousand-mile hike along the Pacific Coast Trail in the far West of the United States. Somewhere out there, she eventually experiences a mental rebirth.

Similar, albeit more tragic, is the movie INTO THE WILD. Here the main character has the curiosity to expose himself to the wild, which allows him to see himself and the world in a whole new way.

A lighter version of self-discovery is EAT PRAY LOVE, in which curiosity sends a woman on a journey of self-discovery and mental happiness throughout Southeast Asia.

It is curiosity that drives most great love stories. One prominent example is the wonderful movie BEFORE SUNRISE. This beautiful story of love, destiny, and soulmates is driven by the two main characters' curiosity to get to know each other more intimately. After a long night spent roaming the streets of Vienna together, they realize they have finally found their soulmate.

Even a surreal Vietnam war movie like APOCALYPSE NOW is driven by its main character's curiosity: The army captain Benjamin L. Willard goes on a mission to find and liquidate a rogue colonel who has built a hidden shadow army deep in the Cambodian jungle. Only when the captain develops a mysterious fascination and curiosity for his target, the elusive Colonel Kurtz, does this dark war tale turn into a true masterpiece.

Stay a little scientist throughout life

Curiosity is important for heroes and for each one of us. Think about it: How can we possibly have a fulfilling life without experiencing and learning new things?

Being conscious that the world is full of hidden treasures makes us curious and eager to explore this planet.

Instead of desperately trying to control our world, we can embrace uncertainty. That gives us a chance to see our lives as an enjoyable quest during which we discover, learn, and grow.

Always remember that new experiences with uncertain outcomes are often the most exciting and memorable moments in our lives: blind dates, sports events, even challenging business presentations. Imagine we always know a certain outcome for those events beforehand. Not very exciting, is it?

Uncertainty and surprise bring more thrills and excitement into our lives than most people realize. It is curiosity that makes us seek out and experience those moments.

On a more universal note, intellectual curiosity is the pivotal driver for human progress. We see this most clearly in geniuses who are always curious. For example, Katharine Johnson, Marie Curie, and Albert Einstein were all curious people. It was passion and curiosity that made them explore their subjects on a granular level, and this eventually led to their profound insights and the progress that now benefits all of us.

One of the crucial ingredients of curiosity is to remain fascinated by what we don't know. Curiosity keeps us open to learn, unlearn, and relearn.

Unfortunately, many of us tend to stop asking questions when we grow older because we fear it might make us look stupid. We don't put ourselves in situations of uncertainty anymore as we are then more vulnerable. By avoiding the unknown and any potential distress, we become less open, and there is a real threat of stagnating and growing anxious.

Just think of the most curious beings on this planet: children. They are like empty canvasses, eagerly waiting to be filled with knowledge and experiences without any fixed expectations. Children between the ages of two and four ask an estimated 40,000 questions of their caregivers. (38)

As unnerving as this might be to the parents, children with their insatiable thirst for knowledge should be a good example for all of us. The famous psychologist Jean Piaget described children as "little scientists," because they are always wondering about things and making their own theories about how the world around them works.

So, let's go out there and release our inner child. Listen to Albert Einstein, who remained eager to learn new things throughout his life. "The important thing is not to stop questioning... Never lose our holy curiosity."

Be a little scientist. Be daring. Be curious. Go and discover something new every day. Heroes do.

FOR THE IMPATIENT AND HURRIED

Three ways to foster our curiosity:

1. ASK QUESTIONS, ALWAYS

Make What, Why, When, Where and How your best friends. Do not take things at face value. Always dig deeper. Ask and ask and ask.

2. DO NOT ASSUME

Do not assume or label something from the outset. Most things can be interesting if we give them a chance.

3. VARY SOURCES OF INFORMATION

Listen to people and publications from a wide variety of backgrounds and beliefs, including those who have viewpoints different from ours.

PART IV

friends and companionship

13 FRIENDS
AND
COMPANIONSHIP

...or why friends are the spice of life

Philippe is now in the last third of his life. He is ridiculously rich and inhabits a luxurious townhouse in Paris with many servants. On the outset, it looks as if he has a dream life, but Philippe is mostly miserable and depressed. Destiny gave him a hard time: He had a paragliding accident and has been quadriplegic ever since. On top of that, his beloved wife died tragically without bearing any children.

So, Philippe lives a life full of self-pity and begrudges his unlucky existence. His only joy seems to be an epistolary relationship with Eleonore, whom he has never met in real life.

One day, when Philippe and his assistant interview potential live-in caregivers for him, the rebellious street criminal on parole, Driss, storms into his life. Driss is one of the candidates for the role but actually has zero interest in getting the job. He is just there to get a signature to show that he applied and got rejected, which will grant him further welfare benefits.

But Philippe likes Driss' energy and the fact that he does not treat him with pity like all the other caregivers. Philippe gives him the job, much to Driss' surprise. Reluctant at first, Driss soon grows into the job and brings some excitement into Philippe's life with unconventional methods and spontaneous parties.

The two form an unlikely but beautiful friendship: The friendship of a disabled white millionaire with a black street criminal who was in jail for robbery. Driss helps Philippe come to terms with his life by confronting his issues head-on. He also encourages Philippe to personally meet his pen pal and secret love, Eleonore, who doesn't know of Philippe's disability.

Philippe, on the other hand, introduces Driss to the finer things in life, such as modern art, opera, and painting and encourages him to sort out the troubles his younger cousin faces with street gangs.

In the end, they part ways, both having been transformed to the better through their unlikely encounter and subsequent friendship. There is a hint that they will remain friends throughout their lives.

This is the story of the beautiful movie THE INTOUCHABLES, based on true events.

The value of companionship

This chapter is not really about a character trait but about companionship every hero ultimately needs and values.

Heroes are social animals like all of us. They value companionship, they meet and lose friends on their journeys, and they work in teams to master adventures they couldn't possibly manage alone. Heroic deeds are more often than not dependent on collaboration.

Admittedly, relationships can be messy. They are often hard to establish and maintain, but the effort usually pays off in the end. Even enemies can turn into helpers. There are challenges on our life journeys that we simply cannot master on our own. Heroes know that and value friends and teamwork.

It is a pearl of old wisdom that a good team is often stronger than the sum of its individual members. A lot of proof about such exponential synergy effects can be taken from history: Think of the Beatles. True, some people believe that John Lennon and Paul McCartney were geniuses on their own. But did they alone achieve even a fraction of the masterpieces they produced with their other band members?

If we look at other rock bands like The Rolling Stones or Pink Floyd, it gets even more apparent that the team was way stronger than its individual parts. Just listen to some of Mick Jagger's solo efforts from the 1980s for a few examples.

Think of the world of business. Take duos like Sergey Brin and Larry Page (Google,) Steve Jobs and Steve Wozniak (Apple,) and Paul Allen and Bill Gates (Microsoft.) They each had a partner and a team around them to achieve such stellar accomplishments in business and technology. Many of the great industrialists and engineers have come in pairs. They found like-minded people who thought and acted in new and original ways.

Also, in the world of politics, the value of a helping hand cannot be underestimated. American hero George Washington depended greatly on his young aide Alexander Hamilton during the Revolutionary War and for a great part of his later career. It was HAMILTON, not Washington, who was eventually eternalized in the highly successful Broadway musical from 2015.

In the world of sports, the value of companionship and teams is even more apparent. Even in non-team sports like tennis or Formula One auto racing, the single athlete is always dependent on the helpers around them.

A team can apply a mix of skills that go beyond the scope of any one individual. Also, a team is more likely to solve complex problems that require more than one mind. The important thing to remember is that the best teams get their mix of personalities just right.

The most magnificent things can occur as a result of team effort, when the team members set aside their selfish interests and focus on accomplishing something collectively that they could not achieve on their own. The political activist Helen Keller, who, as a deaf-blind person, successfully campaigned for women's suffrage and labor rights, said, "Alone we can do so little; together we can do so much."

Old friends stood the test of time

It is true that everybody needs some downtime occasionally and will want to be alone for a while. However, the need for companionship is real. It makes us human, gives us emotional balance, and it lets us enjoy life. According to Maslow's Hierarchy of Needs, the need for "belonging" comes right after the fundamental needs of food, safety, and shelter.

Even if we should make a rational decision with our brain to be on our own and avoid any form of relationship, that other big organ in our chest will always desire a human connection.

Since the dawn of mankind, people, like most animals, have lived in groups. This makes us feel more secure and at ease with the world around us. We form emotional connections in order to express ideas and emotions and get feedback from our tribe.

For a person to be happy, finding the right companions and feeling a sense of belonging are critical. When this need is not being met, we experience psychological discomfort.

And what is one of the best kinds of companionship? It is, of course... friends.

Friends are the backbone of our lives. They are there in good and bad times, they give us a reality check when needed, they listen, they cut the small talk, they give us advice, they encourage us, they continually give us new reasons to be happy, and they are a brilliant soundboard. Most importantly, they get us out of that slump when needed.

We mostly love them. We sometimes hate them. But one thing we cannot deny: They are the spice of our lives. Whether we want to admit it or not, friends are a reflection of us. We are more shaped by our friends than we realize or like to admit. Some psychologists claim that ultimately, we are the average of the five people we hang out with most often.

Especially when we grow old, having close mates is essential. They stood the test of time, and the sheer fact that we kept them over all those years means they somehow contributed to our well-being.

According to a study conducted by researchers at the University of North Carolina at Chapel in 2016, the depth and breadth of our social connections will impact our health as much as diet and exercise. Staggering, isn't it? (39)

We are a social species, hard-wired to form social bonds with other humans; this is a biological requirement that leads to happiness, self-worth and a sense of purpose.

Annoying though they can be, friends ultimately make us happy. Leading experts in the field of happiness research discovered that people with strong relationship ties are generally happier. (40) Even frequent social interaction with weaker relationship ties has a positive effect on our wellbeing. (41)

Beware of group-thinking

Are there any disadvantages to being in a group?

Well, there is a dark side to almost everything. Our best friends, the people who know us best, have the most power to betray us on both intellectual and emotional levels should the relationship sour. Needy friends can get in the way of dealing with more critical issues. Toxic friendships and relationships can suck a lot of energy from us.

The key is: Choose friends wisely. Always pay attention to a gut feeling when meeting new people; it usually makes the right decision. The best friends are commonly those who share our same values. It is the groups and companionships based on the same values that have the strongest ties.

Larger groups, especially, may fall into the psychological phenomena called "group-thinking" and "group-polarization." Group-thinking happens when the group develops its own mind to such a degree so that individual members stop being critical. In group-polarization, some members prove willing to make more extreme decisions than they would have individually.

But the advantages of good friendships and relationships still outweigh the negatives by far.

Friendship can save a hero's life

"Let the rest of the world beat their brains out for a buck. It's friends that count. And I got friends", says the troublesome Broadway star Margo Channing in ALL ABOUT EVE. She has had enough of the quarrels in her life. But there is one comfort left that keeps her getting up in the morning: knowing she has good friends she can rely on. And this is all that matters for her.

Good examples of the importance of a hero's friends and helpers– sometimes called "sidekicks"– are everywhere.

Butch Cassidy rode with The Sundance Kid. Thelma escaped with Louise. The Lone Ranger had Tonto. Harry Potter could rely on Hermione and Ron. Han Solo was saved by Chewbacca. Frodo was carried by Sam up Mount Doom. The list continues...

There are also many teams out there. Remember THE MAGNIFICENT SEVEN, THE DIRTY DOZEN, THE A-TEAM, THE GOONIES, and THE AVENGERS. The list goes on forever.

Friends are an integral part of every Hero's Journey. They are so natural to the hero that they do not need an explanation as to why there are in the story. Remember when Sally said to Harry: "It's so nice when we can sit with someone and not have to talk."

Even a solitary superhero like Batman found a friend in his butler Alfred, and later his cheerful sidekick Robin. The solitary James Bond had a Q and a Felix Leiter he could rely on.

Ironically, it is often not the hero but their friends who make the movie enjoyable. Would SEINFELD be only remotely funny if it weren't for his chaotic buddies Kramer and George?

There is a whole genre dealing with this companionship, called the "buddy movie." Buddy movies might be comedies such as THE BLUES BROTHERS, DUMB AND DUMBER, and WAYNE'S WORLD. They might be action films such as RUSH HOUR, BAD BOYS, and BEVERLY HILLS COP. Sometimes they are dramas such as THE SHAWSHANK REDEMPTION.

Very often, friends are there to help the heroes grow or teach them a life lesson.

LEON: THE PROFESSIONAL is a simple-minded contract killer whose life changes when he makes friends with a neglected neighbor girl. He not only grows as a human through this unlikely friendship but finds a purpose in his aimless life.

Sometimes the hero's friends can be really annoying. Imagine we had a friend who forgets our name every five seconds. Marlin, in FINDING NEMO, finds a friend exactly like that in the depths of the ocean: Dory, the fish with short-term memory loss. But in the end, it is Dory who has the decisive idea of how to find and rescue Marlin's missing son, Nemo.

The hero's friend and helper may come from an entirely different species. Who could forget the heart-wrenching stories of FREE WILLY and LASSIE COME HOME, when a child becomes best friends with an orca and a collie respectively? Both of these animals teach our kid heroes essential life lessons that most adults could not have given them.

One of the most blissful friendships was brought to us by the movie THE LION KING. Timon and Pumbaa, a meerkat and a warthog, are inseparable and chaotically cheerful friends. When Simba, the little lion, wants to join the club, Timon at first doesn't see any merit in befriending a helpless lion cub. It is Pumbaa who convinces Timon that it could be very practical to have a lion in their circle of friends. And very practical it turns out to be, as the lion grows up strong and brave and eventually becomes the hero of that tale, saving the kingdom as well as Timon's and Pumbaa's lives.

Odd friendships can, of course, happen in the worlds of humans, too. The highly acclaimed movie MIDNIGHT COWBOY is the bittersweet tale of an unlikely friendship between a young Texan named Joe and a crippled conman named Ratso. Together they hustle the streets of 1960s Manhattan and go through some peculiar adventures.

In the end, Joe becomes a hero for poor Ratso, a guy who needed a hero if anyone ever did. Joe selflessly gives up on his career as a hustler to fulfil Ratso's dream of going to Miami, and together, they board a bus to Florida. Ratso never makes it there alive but having a friend who cares about him– maybe for the first time– made him temporarily very happy in his otherwise short and loveless life.

Some of the best friendship stories can be found in coming-of-age movies. This is mainly because, in our formative years, we make friends with no filters. We don't care about backgrounds but befriend people for the sake of befriending them. We make friends with people we would never meet in our adult years. SUPERBAD, THE PERKS OF BEING A WALLFLOWER, and STAND BY ME are all about these oddly beautiful teenage friendships.

At the end of STAND BY ME, the protagonist and narrator has now grown up and long lost touch with his old friends from childhood. Wistfully he looks back and says, "I never had any friends later on like the ones I had when I was twelve. Jesus, does anyone?"

Even when there are no other people around, the hero may still look for companionship. Think of Chuck, lost on an island in CAST AWAY, who becomes best friends with a volleyball called Wilson. Robert is a lonely prisoner in BIRDMAN OF ALCATRAZ, who makes friends with an orphaned baby sparrow.

Everybody knows something we don't

Companionships. Friendships. Teams. We have seen that they are essential in every story as well as in every life.

Having friends who understand us, and who contribute to our lives with all their bluntness and imperfections, is a blessing beyond measure. Heroes need them, and so do the rest of us.

Humans are amongst the most complex and fascinating species on this planet. Everybody has a new story to tell. Everybody we meet knows something we don't. And they can all open new doors for us and makes this beautiful world just a little bit bigger.

Ever notice how easy it is for small children to make new friends? That's because they don't overthink it. Judgment and critical reasoning do not get in their way. They trust their instincts.

So, go out there and revitalize some lost friendships. Then develop some new ones. We are all living on borrowed time, and we will be remembered not only for what we did in life, but especially for whom we touched throughout our journey.

As the famous choreographer Twyla Tharp said: "What we are today and what we will be in five years depend on two things: the people we meet and the books we read."

True words.

Also, listen to the Spanish philosopher Baltasar Gracian, who said: "Friendship multiplies the good of life and divides the evil."

Simply put, good friendships and social contacts are some of the best stuff in life. Go out and foster them. Heroes do.

FOR THE IMPATIENT AND HURRIED

Three ways to choose the right friends:

1. CHOOSE FRIENDS WITH SIMILAR VALUES TO YOUR OWN.

Friends with similar values keep us accountable and will not expect us to compromise on the values that govern our lives.

2. CHOOSE FRIENDS WITH COMPLEMENTARY SKILLS.

Friends who have skills in areas we don't have can teach us, stretch us, and challenge us... and vice versa.

3. LISTEN TO YOUR GUT

When we first meet someone, our gut normally tells us the right thing. Listen to it.

CONCLUSION

So, that's it. I hope you enjoyed the ride. Remember in the beginning when I said that this is not a self-help book? I don't think it is. I am a bit wary of self-help books, as I have found them generally too formulaic and absolute in their statements. As if one book could let us master this complex and erratic beast called life. I don't think it could.

But I do believe that people learn from examples, stories, and, of course, heroes. Though we each have to take the journey ourselves, heroes and their journeys can point us in the right direction. And I hope that somewhere in this book, you might have found a little inspiration for a new direction.

I don't expect anybody to go out now and instantly become a hero. Remember that heroism is often situational. And, to be quite frank, I am not sure I would want any of us to come into a situation where we have to act heroically as it could potentially be life-threatening to us.

What I do want, though, is that no one ever underestimates their shapeshifting abilities. Humans are an extremely adaptable, resilient, and flexible species. If we put our minds to it, we can become pretty much anything we want at any stage in our lives. Often, we need to act out the role we want to be until we slowly but surely become it. I believe in that. After all, heroes are made, not born; they start ordinary and only become what they are on their journey.

If there's only one thing to take away from this book, it's this: A good life doesn't mean an easy one. Often it is quite the opposite.

A recent study by philosopher Lorraine Besser of Middlebury College and psychologist Shigehiro Oishi of the University of Virginia found that people value a "psychologically rich" life more than they value a "happy" life. (42) A psychologically rich life is one that is full of varied emotions and surprises, including setbacks and seemingly negative emotions like grief, anger, and shame.

And that is the point. If there is one thing all tales of heroes have in common, it is that they are never easy. The Hero's Journey is always filled with varied emotions and setbacks, often including fear, grief and sorrow.

The beauty is that we are transformed through rich experience and the struggles we live through. At one point of our journey, we might come to the realization that we are more than we thought we were. And, in the end, there is a good chance that we will see the world differently and often closer to what it really is. Quite remarkable considering that nothing has changed apart from us, isn't it?

I firmly believe that, in a rich life, the sweet spot is found in the interface of good ideas and good people. That's why we should create a family with someone we love. Form a rock band with people we like to hang out with. Start a business with somebody we admire. The venture might not always end with our desired outcome, but if we do it with the right forte and portion of enthusiasm, there is a high likelihood that these endeavors will enrich our lives regardless.

We must seek experiences that leave us feeling fully alive. We must take risks. Life is not linear but organic. All we can do is to take the first step and plunge right into it. Feeling lost at the start of the journey is normal and part of the game. Embrace it. Often a Hero's Journey starts with the loss of the familiar, the loss of the comfort of our known surroundings. If life were a washing machine, embarking on a Hero's Journey would be the spin cycle.

And wouldn't it be great if we did something, we had told ourselves we could never do– but yet we did? Even *attempting* the impossible can have a transformative effect on us, whether we succeed or not. After all, it is not about winning or losing but about staying true to ourselves.

There is a misconception that we can only help this planet by doing something ground-breaking or game changing. I do not think that is true. If we live an authentic life and follow our journey from the heart, our lives will be more vital, and so will we.

Vital people vitalize. We are always an example for somebody. We are always teaching something, whether we intend to or not. If more people live their life authentically and follow their bliss, this good energy will be passed on and create ripple effects. The world will become a better place by definition. Never forget the ripple effect. It is real.

And never expect life to unfold the way we planned it to. Make bold and risky moves. Some people seem to refuse the loan of life to avoid the debt of death. This is like going on a vacation and avoiding friendships because the vacation will be over at some point. That doesn't make sense.

I would like to close this book with an old anecdote that struck a chord with me. It comes from Joseph Campbell himself.

Quite some time ago, Campbell attended a conference on religion in Japan. There he overheard one of the American delegates inquiring something of an elderly Shinto priest. The delegate told the Japanese priest that he had seen their shrines and ceremonies, but still did not understand their ideology and theology.

The Japanese priest thought for a while and then responded: "I think we don't have ideology. We don't have theology. We dance."

And maybe this is it. Maybe we should dance without knowing the tune. Maybe we shouldn't be too hung up with rigid plans. Maybe we should not label our lives in a manner that any deviation from that label makes us unhappy. Maybe we should accept all the unexpected twists and turns that life throws at us and dance with them.

So, go out now and dance. Heroes do.

CODA

It is November 2020. I'm sitting here in my flat in South London, overlooking some beautifully arranged gardens illuminated by the evening sun of this pretty English autumn.

Meanwhile, COVID-19 has grabbed the whole world and shaken it severely. Things will never be the same again. I cannot stop thinking of all the people out there going through a much tougher journey in 2020 than they envisioned they would last New Year's Day.

But I was also delighted to see how adaptable and resilient people can be when hit unprepared by a crisis. It proves my point that crises often bring out the best in people. I've seen a lot of solidarity and volunteering out there. Indeed, I believe that we will come out a stronger and better society on the other end of this.

I also believe this crisis will spawn a lot of new heroes. In the end, heroism is situational, and it turned out that there were many heroes-in-waiting out there who have now found an opportunity to do their heroic deeds.

COVID-19 showed yet again that the quality of our lives depends on collaboration and not competitiveness. Heroes always act in cooperation and try to improve the greater good. The hero is not the dude who jumps from the stratosphere with a parachute, sponsored by an energy drink company. No, the hero is the person who sits all day on a supermarket cash register and risks being infected with the virus while providing other people with essential supplies.

COVID-19 destroyed a lot of business for me. But on a positive note, it gifted me quality time with my parents and wiped out all excuses I had not to finish this book.

If you are reading this, then I did finally decide to publish this book. I initially started writing it for myself to clarify my thoughts about heroes and their impact on us. But then it got longer. And longer. And longer. And I foolishly gave the manuscript to some friends, and they said, well, it might be worth getting it out there.

Some of them inquired of me as to whether I myself adopt the hero's characteristics that I write about and, through that, live the life I always wanted. Does the preacher follow his own sermons?

I had to think about that. The answer is that I try to do so every day, even though my life is not the one I had envisioned for myself. Throughout my early life, I wanted to become a movie director and live with my big family in Hollywood. Nothing of that ever materialized.

Instead, I live on my own on the other side of the world in South London, where I teach, consult, and write. Have I have ever regretted that my life did not go the way I wanted it to? Yes, quite often. And sometimes, on dark winter nights, I still do.

But does that mean I do not like my current life? No, absolutely not. It is just different. I might have gotten a bit side-tracked by some threshold guardians, and maybe I was not brave enough in some pivotal situations, but overall it is a great life.

I met some great people on my journey, lived through some good and bad times, and saw quite a few stunning places on this beautiful planet called Earth. I only stumbled into teaching by chance, and now I think I was not all that bad at it. I realized how rewarding it is to teach others and help them on their journey... so I stuck with it.

As for my movie dreams, I'm not entirely done with them yet. Through researching and writing this book, I got encouraged to give it a go. Writing can have a therapeutic effect, they say. I can wholeheartedly confirm that, and, so, I decided to direct my first feature film on a micro-budget next year. I might fail miserably, but that's not the point, is it?

More recently, I tried to send Molly – remember Molly, from the Introduction? – the first copy of this book. After all, she is the reason why this book exists.

But I couldn't locate her. Internet searches with her name

didn't yield any proper results, apart from an arty Flickr photo stream from 2011. I found this strange, as we would assume that most business post-graduates from a prestigious school would at least have a LinkedIn account. But Molly wasn't like most graduates, and she didn't have one.

Next, I went to the alumni office to inquire about her whereabouts. They were reluctant at first because they cannot give out personal data; but when I explained the situation and begged a bit, they tried to look up Molly for me and... nothing. They could only tell me that she is originally from Limerick, Ireland.

Very strange, I thought. Maybe Molly doesn't want to be found? I'd like to believe that she embarked on her own Hero's Journey and escaped the predicament called 2020. And, yes, maybe she did make it to the Antarctic and is counting penguins now. I'll bet that *that* part of the world is still virus-free. And I'll bet Molly uses her time wisely to hang out with cheerful feathered company and enjoys plenty of quality introspection time.

I'm so sorry, Molly, that I couldn't find you, but I trust you're on the right path wherever you might be. And if you do happen to read this book, please let me know if it answered all your questions.

For everybody else: If you have any comments or further thoughts, if you found inspiration or anything else in this book– or if you bumped into Molly by chance– I would like to hear from you. I really would. nico@universalstoryteller.co.uk

So long... and keep dancing through this mystery called life.

Nico, London, November 2020

ACKNOWLEDGEMENTS

I would like to thank the following brilliant academics, psychologists, hero scientists & practitioners who granted me their time with insightful interviews:

Dr. Elaine Kinsella, University of Limerick, Psychologist
Elizabeth Svoboda, Science Writer, Author of "What makes a hero?"
Freya de Meleghy, Psychotherapist in practice, Trauma specialist
Dr. Olivia Efthimiou, Murdoch University, Heroism Scientist
Prof. Ari Kohen, University of Nebraska-Lincoln, Professor of Social Justice
Clive Williams, Psychotherapist in practice, Author of "A mudmap for heroes"
Matt Langdon, Founder of the Hero Construction Company

I would like to thank Janeen Sloan for doing a tremendous job of copy-editing this book, and Maite Lantaron for the beautiful illustrations and lay-out.

And, of course, I would like to thank all my friends who read this book on various stages and gave me invaluable insights, criticism, and suggestions. Without your nagging and continuous encouragement, this book would have never come to be (in random order):

Ron Kellermann, Julissa Lopez-Hodoyan, Leandro D'Andrea, Mark Batistich, Sasha Tando, Kelechi Okoro, Mark Whittington, Rasha Albazaz, Tom van Laer, Huma Farooqui, Nat Darke, Richard Nield, Simon Rilling, Sean O'Reilly, Kasia Iwakoshi, Gudula Schinke, Martina Zacharopoulous, Silke Schrupp, Clelia Clini, Francesco Arzilli, Allon Zloof, Niklas Gebele, Jörn Radloff, Paul Sakey, Jon Cartwright, Paddy Bird, Campbell Taylor.

BIBLIOGRAPHY

WHAT IS A HERO

(1) Scott T. Allison, George R.Goethals, *Heroes: What They Do and Why We Need them* (Oxford: OUP USA, 2010)

(2) Philip Zimbardo, What Makes a Hero? (Presentation at the Greater Good Science Center at the University of California, Berkeley, 2011)

Further Reading:

Joseph Campbell, *The Hero with A Thousand Faces (The Collected Works of Joseph Campbell)*, (Novato: New World Library, 2012)

Philip Zimbardo, *The Lucifer Effect: How Good People Turn Evil,* (London: Rider, 2008)

Christopher Vogler, *Writer's Journey: Mythic Structure for Writers,* (Studio City: Michael Wiese Production, 2007)

PROACTIVITY

(3) Shai Davidai, Thomas Gilovich, "*The Ideal Road Not Taken: The Self-Discrepancies Involved in People's Most Enduring Regrets*", Emotion, Vol. 18, No. 3, 439–452, American Psychological Association, 2018

Further reading:

Mark Manson, *The Subtle Art of Not Giving a F*ck: A Counterintuitive Approach to Living a Good Life*, (New York: Harper, 2016)

SELF-DETERMINATION

(4) Clive Williams, *A Mudmap for Living: A practical guide to daily living based on Joseph Campbell's The Hero Journey, (Australia, Dr. Clive Williams, 2016)*

(5) Francesca Gino, Scott S. Wiltermuth, "*Evil Genius? How Dishonesty Can Lead to Greater Creativity*", Psychological Science, vol. 25, 4: pp. 973- 981, First Published February 18, 2014.

(6) Zhen Zhang,, Richard D. Arvey, "*Rule breaking in adolescence and entrepreneurial status: An empirical investigation*", Journal of Business Venturing 24 (2009) 436–447

Further reading:

Hannah Arendt, *The Origins of Totalitarianism*, (London: Penguin Classics, 2017)

Rosa Parks, *My Story*, (London: Puffin, 1999)

GRIT

(7) Angela Duckworth, *Grit: The Power of Passion and Perseverance*, (New York: Scribner Book Company (2016)

(8) Malcolm Gladwell, *Outliers: The Story of Success*, (London: Penguin Books, 2009)

Further reading:

Angela Duckworth: Grit: *The Power of Passion and Perseverance*, (New York: Scribner Book Company (2016)

Ernest Hemingway, *The old man and the sea*, (London: Arrow, 1994)

POSITIVITY

(9) Lawrence J. Walker, Jeremy A. Frimer, William L. Dunlop, *"Varieties of Moral Personality: Beyond the Banality of Heroism"*, Journal of Personality, Volume 78, Issue 3, 12 May, 2010

(10) Elise K Kalokerinos, William von Hippel, Julie D Henry, Robert Trivers, *"The aging positivity effect and immune function: Positivity in recall predicts higher CD4 counts and lower CD4 activation,"* Psychology and aging, Volume 29, Issue 3, 2014/9

(11) Srivastava, S., McGonigal, K. M., Richards, J. M., Butler, E. A., & Gross, J. J., *"Optimism in close relationships: How seeing things in a positive light makes them so"*, Journal of Personality and Social Psychology, 91(1), 143–153, 2006

(12) Kate Sweeny, James Shepperd, *"The costs of optimism and the benefits of pessimism"*, Emotion, 10(5), 750–753, 2010

(13) Emmons, R. A., & McCullough, M. E., *"Counting blessings versus burdens: An experimental investigation of gratitude and subjective well-being in daily life"*, Journal of Personality and Social Psychology, 84(2), 377–389, 2003

Further reading:

Carol S. Dweck, *Mindset: How You Can Fulfil Your Potential*, (London: Robinson, 2012)

Norman Vincent Peale, *The power of positive thinking*, (New York, Touchstone, 1992)

STOICISM

(14) Junchol Park, Jesse Wood, Corina Bondi, Alberto Del Arco and Bita Moghaddam, *Anxiety Evokes Hypofrontality and Disrupts Rule-Relevant Encoding by Dorsomedial Prefrontal Cortex Neurons, Journal of Neuroscience*, 36 (11) 3322-33316, March 2016

Further reading:

Marcus Aurelius, *Meditations*, (Basingstoke: Macmillan Collector's Library, 2020)

Ryan Holliday, *The Obstacle is the Way: The Ancient Art of Turning Adversity to Advantage*, (London: Profile Books, 2014)

INTEGRITY

(15) Martin E.P. Seligman, *Flourish: a visionary new understanding of happiness and well-being*, (New York, Toronto: Free Press, 2012)

Further reading:

Nelson Mandela: *Long Walk To Freedom: The Autobiography of Nelson Mandela*, (London: Abacus, 1995)

Tillar J. Mazzeo: *Irena's Children: The Extraordinary Story of the Woman Who Saved 2,500 Children from the Warsaw Ghetto*, (New York: Gallery, 2009)

PURPOSEFULNESS

(16) Barbara L. Fredrickson, Karen M. Grewen, Kimberly A. Coffey, Sara B. Algoe, Ann M. Firestine, Jesusa M. G. Arevalo, Jeffrey Ma, and Steven W. Cole, *A functional genomic perspective on human well-being*, PNAS, 110 (33) 13684-13689, August 13, 2013

(17) Viktor E. Frankl, Man's search for meaning, (Boston: Beacon Press, 2006)

(18) Irvin Yalom, *Staring at the sun: Overcoming the terror of death*, (San Francisco: Jossey-Bass, 2009)

Further reading:

Ken Robinson: *The Element: How Finding Your Passion Changes Everything*, (London: Penguin, 2009)

Edith Eger, *The Choice: A true story of hope*, (London: Rider, 2018)

ALTRUISM

(19) Allan Luks, *"Helper's high: Volunteering makes people feel good, physically and emotionally."* Psychology Today, 22(10), 34-42, 1988

(20) Michael J. Poulin, Stephanie L. Brown, Amanda J. Dillard, Dylan M.Smith, *"Giving to Others and the Association Between Stress and Mortality"*, American Journal of Public Health 103, no. 9, pp. 1649-1655, 2013

(21) Rodolfo Cortes Barragan, Carol S. Dweck, *"Reciprocity triggers children's benevolence"*, Proceedings of the National Academy of Sciences, 111 (48) 17071-17074, Dec. 2014

(22) Elizabeth Svoboda, *What makes a hero*, (New York: Current, 2013)

(23) Philip Zimbardo, *What Makes a Hero?* (Presentation at the Greater Good Science Center at the University of California, Berkeley, 2011)

Further reading:

Matthieu Ricard, *Altruism: The Power of Compassion to Change Yourself and the World*, (London: Atlantic Books, 2015)

Stefan Klein, *Survival of the Nicest: How Altruism Made Us Human and Why It Pays to Get Along*, (New York: Experiment, 2015)

RESPONSIBILITY

(24) Catherine E. Ross, John Mirowsky, *"The Sense of Personal Control: Social Structural Causes and Emotional Consequences"* In: Aneshensel C.S., Phelan J.C., Bierman A. (eds) Handbook of the Sociology of Mental Health. Handbooks of Sociology and Social Research, (Dordrecht: Springer, 2012)

(25) John Darley, Bibb Latane, *"Bystander intervention in emergencies: Diffusion of responsibility"*, Journal of Personality and Social Psychology, 8(4, Pt.1), 377-383, 1968

Further reading:

Chesley Sullenberger, *Highest Duty: My Search for What Really Matters*, (New York: William Morrow Paperbacks, 2010)

Mohandas Karamchand Gandhi, *An Autobiography: The Story of My Experiments with Truth*, (London: Penguin Classics, 2001)

COURAGE

(26) Research conducted by Statistic Brain Research Institute, 2016, https://www.statisticbrain.com/fear-of-public-speaking-statistics/

(27) Joseph Campbell, The Hero with A Thousand Faces (The Collected Works of Joseph Campbell), (Novato: New World Library, 2012)

(28) Mark R. Leary. Emotional responses to interpersonal rejection. *Dialogues Clin Neurosci*;17(4):435-441, 2015

Further reading:

Joseph Murphy: *The Power Of Your Subconscious Mind*, (London: Penguin, 2011)

Brené Brown, *Daring Greatly: How the Courage to Be Vulnerable Transforms the Way We Live, Love, Parent, and Lead,* (New York: Avery, 2015)

Rollo May, *The courage to create*, (New York: W. W. Norton & Company, 1994)

SHADOWS

(29) Stephen A. Diamond, *"Shadow"*, In: Leeming D.A., Madden K., Marlan S. (eds) Encyclopedia of Psychology and Religion. Springer, Boston, MA, 2010

(30) Jennifer D. Shapka, Shereen Khan, *"Self-Perception"*, In: Levesque R.J.R. (eds) Encyclopedia of Adolescence. Springer, Cham, 2018

(31) Robert Bly, *A Little Book on the Human Shadow* (Australia: HarperCollins, 1988)

Further reading:

Connie Zweig, *Meeting the Shadow: The Hidden Power of the Dark Side of Human Nature*, (New York: TarcherPerigee, 1991)

Carl G Jung, *The Archetypes and The Collective Unconscious*, (Princeton: Princeton University Press, 1981)

CURIOSITY

(32) Todd B. Kashdan, Paul Rose & Frank D. Fincham, *"Curiosity and Exploration: Facilitating Positive Subjective Experiences and Personal Growth Opportunities"*, Journal of Personality Assessment, 82:3, 291-305, 2004

(33) Gary E. Swan., Dorit Carmelli, *"Curiosity and mortality in aging adults: A 5-year follow-up of the Western Collaborative Group Study"* Psychology and Aging, 11(3), 449–453, 1996

(34) Matthias J. Gruber,Bernard D. Gelman,Charan Ranganath, *"States of Curiosity Modulate Hippocampus-Dependent Learning via the*

Dopaminergic Circuit", Neuron, Elsevier, 2014

(35) Mihaly Csikszentmihalyi, *Creativity: Flow and the Psychology of Discovery and Invention* (New York: Harper Perennial, 2013)

(36) Todd Kashdan, Michael Steger, *"Curiosity and pathways to well-being and meaning in life: Traits, states, and everyday behaviors"*, Motivation and Emotion. 31. 159-173

(37) Hsee, Christopher & Ruan, Bowen, *"The Pandora Effect: The Power and Peril of Curiosity"*, Psychological Science. 27. 10.1177, 2016

(38) Paul L. Harris, *"Trusting What You're Told How Children Learn from Others"*, (Cambridge: Belknap Press, 2005)

Further reading about Curiosity:

Brian Grazer, *Curious Mind: The Secret to a Bigger Life* (New York: Simon & Schuster, 2015)

Ian Leslie, *Curious: The Desire to Know and Why Your Future Depends on It*, (London: Quercus, 2015)

COMPANIONSHIP

(39) Claire Yang, Courtney Boen, Karen Gerken, Ting Li, Kristen Schorpp, Kathleen Mullan Harris, *"Social relationships and physiological functioning, Proceedings of the National Academy of Sciences"*, 113 (3) 578-583, Jan 2016

(40) Julia Rohrer, David Richter, Martin Brümmer, Gert Wagner, Stefan Schmukle, *"Successfully Striving for Happiness: Socially Engaged Pursuits Predict Increases in Life Satisfaction"*, Psychological Science, 29(8):1291-1298, 2018

(41) Gillian M. Sandstrom, Elizabeth W. Dunn, *"Social Interactions and Well-Being: The Surprising Power of Weak Ties"* Personality and Social Psychology Bulletin, 40(7):910-922, 2014

Further reading:

Lydia Denworth, *Friendship: The Evolution, Biology, and Extraordinary Power of Life's Fundamental Bond*, (New York: W. W. Norton & Company, 2020)

Aminatou Sow, Ann Friedman, *Big Friendship: How We Keep Each Other Close*, (London: Virago, 2020)

CONCLUSION

(42) Lorraine L. Besser, Shigehiro Oishi, *"The psychologically rich life"* Philosophical Psychology, 33:8,1053-1071, 2020

INDEX

T

U

V

For a heroic journey of another kind check out my children's book **'The Little Asteroid'**.

Printed in Great Britain
by Amazon

58186732R00106